THE CATASTROPHIC DECLINE OF AMERICA'S PUBLIC HIGH SCHOOLS: NEW YORK CITY, A CASE STUDY

By Jeffrey Ludwig

TABLE OF CONTENTS

PREFACE

This book is divided into an Introduction and five Parts. Each Part is divided into Mini-Chapters. The formal conception of the book is comparable to expressionism in painting, namely to depict a sense of the passion and underlying emotional connections – while at the same time capturing and delineating the "realistic" features of the scene. Thus, its goal is not mere "realism" as in Van Eyck or Rembrandt, but to get a sense of reality in motion as with Edvard Munch, Egon Schiele, El Greco, or even their pre-cursor among the impressionists, Van Gogh (I'm thinking of his Starry Starry Night).

This author is striving to escape from the hackneyed and trite types of writings which simply package ten problems and provide some formulaic five-point (or more points) solution. Here we want to depict a sense of the problems facing education…suggestions for repairing the situation, yet at the same time a sense that the problems have gone too far, that the so-called reforms that are now on the table and being widely accepted are creating more problems than they are solving, and that movement forward depends a lot on our ability to "move back" to recover aspects of culture/education that have been discarded over preceding decades. There must also be a revived dependence upon Almighty God as part of a mix of strategies/applications that will be truly effective.

Jeffrey Ludwig 2014

INTRODUCTION

Education in the United States is imploding. It is clear to everyone that the idea of going to school to 'make something of yourself', to become a leader of a society, to advance one's ability to make a living, to grow in knowledge, manners, or even, at one time, to grow in godliness are diluted and/or abolished from education. The ideals of the Horatio Alger books depicting the conditions for successful fulfillment of one's ambitions have been superseded. Even where we have hard work, the work ethic is eerily absent (slaves or deprived/oppressed peoples may work hard, but cannot be said to uphold the work *ethic*). The weaknesses, failures, and ultimately the path of doom that we find in education has not been and cannot be remediated by the measures of so-called reform taken during the past twenty-five years. These include outcome-based education, school-to-work concepts and laws, influx of federal moneys to an unprecedented degree under No Child Left Behind and Common Core implementations, standardized testing across the curricula, new teacher evaluation frameworks à la Danielson and others, changes to the length of the school day, or the number of years the youth spend in school.

The catastrophic situation we find is a result of a calamitous breakdown in the Weltanschauung (worldview) guiding the direction and daily context of our educational enterprises. This calamitous breakdown is reflective of a breakdown of similar scope and depth in the social, political spiritual, economic, and intellectual life of our country. Even as early as 1977, Christopher Lasch alerted us to the widespread narcissism growing at an exponential rate in society.[1] Further, federal involvement via the setting up of a Department of Education was portrayed as dangerous even fifty years before Lasch's book by the great Princeton professor, J. Grescham Machen.[2] Further, one does not have to be a professor to see that every moral standard in society is collapsing. Goodness and Judeo-Christian values are openly mocked everyday on TV, in the

---

[1] Christopher Lasch, The Culture of Narcissism: American Life in an Age of Diminishing Expectations, W. W. Norton & Company; Revised edition (May 17, 1991)

[2] Dr. Machen testified before the U. S. Congress in February 1926, opposing the formation of a Federal Department of Education on the grounds that uniformity in education under central control would be a disaster. He argued that education is not a matter of the State, but should be left to each child's parents to educate their children as they please. He prophesied the trend we are now seeing, that uniformity in education always leads to the lowest common denominator.

movies, and, yes, in our schools (there will be a lot more about this in this book).

Once prayer was removed from the schools[3], schools became one-stop social agencies in many cases, the family began to decline as the building block of society, *in loco parentis* gave way to the reverse formula where families are called upon to support the mission of the schools instead of schools supporting the mission of the family, disruptive behavior in the schools increased exponentially, testing began to be an alternative to education rather than simply a part of the educational process, rubrics forced on teachers and students took away from more wholistic conceptions of the subject matter, the grade book became public (all grades having to be published on the Internet) thereby undermining some of the teacher's authority, control, technology and social networking began competing with "education" for the attention of the students as far as their understanding of what meaningful "knowledge" is, and patriotism became *de rigueur* as a motivator for

---

[3] The meaning of the First Amendment "establishment clause" changed over several decades, but prayer in the public schools was abolished in the cases of Engel v. Vitale (1962), Murray v. Curlett (1963), and Abington County School District v. Schempp (1963).
www.allabouthistory.org Copyright 2002-2014.

school spirit and learning/careers. We find ourselves in a situation where student focus on the curricula and the teachers has become diluted. Then add the new "informality" ('give me five' men-tality), the sense of entitlement that many of the young feel and express (encouraged throughout most grades by the "self esteem" school of Maslowian psychology masquerading as 'self actualization'), and growing laziness and we have a very difficult situation indeed.

Also, when did you last hear the words knowledge, passion, dedication, creativity, enthusiasm, hope, orderliness, competence, and respect used to evaluate teachers and schools? For many people, cultural literacy is out-of-date, and the idea of teaching great books for the values and inspiration they impart, is desired by only a few upscale private schools. Increasing numbers of classical private schools have opened over the decades to improve the intellectual life of the students as well as include prayer. Educational values have deteriorated so much that these classical schools have had to go back to medieval models of education, namely the quadrivium and trivium, in order to institute something that looks like an intelligent, purposeful curriculum.[4] The way of thinking we are confronted with is a direct result of the new zeal for statistics, systems, savings and software, and with federal government- driven parameters for "reform" rather than local control.

System reorganization pretends to have as its highest goal 'efficiency.' However, we see social engineering now at the center of all educational reform. Whether at the local level or, as is now more and more the case, at the federal level (Race to the Top moneys to support Common Core), the meta-purpose is a new social engineering whereby the individual teacher, the individual student, or even the individual principal is moved away from center stage. A new meta-control by the master puppeteers of management design and software curriculum creators is the basis for a new part-nership. The individual actors or roles within the individual schools become supporting cast, so to

---

[4] Classical education is comprised of the seven liberal arts which are divided into the Trivium and the Quadrivium. The Trivium subjects are grammar, dialectic, and rhetoric while the Quadrivium includes arithmetic, geometry, music, and astronomy.
http://towardthequadrivium.com/?page_id=191

speak, for the overarching goals set by this partnership.

Quarrels will arise between different versions of this meta-partnership, just as there were differences within communism between the Mensheviks and the Bolsheviks, or between the Trotskyites and the Stalinists. There were differences between communists about the role of the peasants v. the role of the industrial workers (proletariat). There were even differences between Marx and Engels about the role of the family in a communist state. And there were differences between fascists and their co-totalitarian first cousins, the communists, about the extent to which there should be government ownership. The communist totalitarians wanted the abolition of private property; whereas, their fascistic counterparts believed that capital accumulation and "ownership" at the corporate level was still legitimate as long as it was highly controlled (at a level beyond mere regulation) by the all-knowing, all powerful, pervasive powers of the government.

Thus, there continue to be quarrels between the master puppeteers of management design and the political apparatchiks who work with them in devising these meta-controls on public education.

Michael Bloomberg and William "Bill" DiBlasio are successive mayors of New York City. Both are statists. Both believe that the government should organize most facets of human experience and suppress individualism in the schools and other segments of society. But DiBlasio hates the rich. For him, it is a moral, economic, and political imperative that the rich be maligned, disparaged, and rejected to show the validity of "people power." For Bloomberg, the rich have a place within the new statist system he envisages. They might to some degree be marginalized, but should not be suppressed or unduly taxed. Yet, that should not distract the intelligent reader of contemporary life from seeing that DiBlasio and Bloomberg are essentially in the same camp.

But this book is more traditional in outlook. We look back to the years before approximately 1975 when the individual student was at the center. The reformers of today complain that the student was never the center of attention in the schools. They complain *ad infinitum* that the schools were teacher-centered; yet consistently fail to see that the paternalism implied by the teacher-centered classroom – a direct result of the *in loco parentis* legal concept – meant that the teacher as well as the parent stood in front of his or her students as an advocate for that student, someone putting the best interests of the child first. The post-Spockean autonomous child is not in a position to learn autonomously because he or she is not in a position to autonomously establish educational goals for himself or herself. The potential of the child cannot be known by the child, nor can he or she know what is needed in the future. However, now that the self-directed child concept has been let out of the bag (or Pandora's box), it would be very difficult if not impossible to put said false idea(s) back in the box.

The pre-1970's student was encouraged to compete, and also to cooperate. The discipline of the schools was enforced, and in that context of Golden Rule discipline was true cooperation. Helping others through service projects, through saying thank you and please, by speaking respect-fully to teachers and school authorities was a given. Cooperation had a structure. There was a place for you within the moving-forward context of school life as long as you were not a troublemaker. Even if you failed, you had the dignity of knowing you still belonged. Why can't we proceed on a basis where research, character development of students, a great pro-teacher environment (let's celebrate teachers, not talk about whipping them into shape), and the joy of learning are central, where students and schools progress under a realistic curriculum based on knowledge, not on bogus data-driven [sic] parameters? However, sadly, the time to pay the piper is fast approaching....

This book contains comments on contemporary trends in educational policy, personal experiences teaching in New York City's high schools expressed allegorically as well as literally, review of the influence of contemporary leftist thinking as it applies to the humanities and our educational institutions, and personal philosophical observations about the nature of education and of teaching as a vocation.

This book may be too diffuse for some tastes. The suggestions about teaching and about what is right and wrong about education and reform of education will not be sufficiently programmatic for many. But this writer sees chaos and impending doom in education. Plans for improving education too often are, as a former colleague of mine often said, cosmetic. Even the widespread use of technology to provide the students with computers and new software to facilitate learning, while useful, merely creates an appearance of structure over a dumbing down and settling into mediocrity or worse...total contempt for and disintegration of learning and mental process for the vast majority of people. Yet, this serves the agenda of the master puppeteers of management design and software curriculum producers. They will tighten their controls and the dependence of others who are struggling in the schools.[5]

Chaos always leads to more dictatorial controls in order to combat the chaos, but in the schools, the instruments of that dictatorial control are more complex – not just some guys with clubs to come beat people into submission. A great network of controls, so-called evaluations of teachers and

---

[5] For a comprehensive and well written review of studies showing the weak or non-existent results of almost all reform approaches in recent years, I refer the reader to Robert Weissberg, *Bad Students Not Bad Schools*, Transaction Publishers, April 1, 2010.

"individualized computer programs" (like the new iZone educational software) reverse all known educational parameters. The test drives the course, instead of student mastery of the course being tested by the test. Actually, the test results that are desired drive the course. For the cohort of schools in which I taught, New York State Regents' (standardized state tests) were to be 85/85, meaning that 85% of the students would score 85 or higher in the exams. Then the scoring of the tests and the writing of the tests were set up to make that outcome more likely. Certain questions that students were likely to have correct were given more points, and other questions called "scaffolding questions" were actual give-aways. Thus, tests were constructed and modified on an as-needed basis in order to provide certain pre-ordained outcomes. Then the courses were structured to attend primarily to these pre-ordained-outcomes tests (leaving teacher autonomy out of the picture), and thereby education becomes dumbed down, more and more each succeeding year.

The teacher becomes an assistant to the standardized test (scoring parameters) and to the computer rather than the computer being a tool for teaching. Recently, this writer was told about a teacher who was reprimanded in a laboratory for not having her Smartboard turned on during the class even though the students were engaged in hands-on laboratory activities. She was soundly (I almost wrote "smartly") rebuked in front of the entire class.

The teachers are evaluated and rated by the students instead of the teachers evaluating and grading the students. The principal gets control [sic] of his own budget, but every item in the budget is dictated/allocated before the budget reaches him or her. Hiring is done by principals, but the guidelines for hiring must be adhered to or the principal will get a lower rating, and the guidelines have little flexibility or variability even though they are complex. In fact, there is an attempt throughout the education systems to re-define freedom of choice with complexity. The parameters allowed for making the decisions become so complex that in an attempt to figure out the directives, one gets a sense of exercising one's 'freedom' while being forced into conformity. ***Complexity gives the illusion of freedom while denying freedom.***

So, inevitably, this book will appear negative to many as well as insufficiently constructive. Yet, dear reader, **without beginning with the problem, in its truth and darkness, how can one ever hope to come up with a solution?** Yes, where will you begin if you do not see the dire straits we are in as a society? If you begin with a simple point like "I want to improve instruction in this or that subject," or "I want to improve the learning of a particular sub-cultural entity," or "I want to make sure that more kids graduate," then you will have failed to see the big picture and will be flooded ultimately by despair and failure. The big picture is that every good that has ever happened in American education is being reversed with the false claim that that education was a failure, that it failed various minority communities, that it has caused us to lag behind other countries in our skills and knowledge, and that it has failed to create the kind of social commitment and cohesion that we need as a society. All of these are false statements being put forward by manipulators of social institutions and con-sciousness in the name of real progress and in order to replace individual consciousness with collective consciousness, group think to supersede independent individual thinking.

Conservative and liberal legislators are on board together with Common Core – an attempt to impose national standards on our schools. This is a brainchild of earlier legislation passed during the Bush years known as No Child Left Behind. That legislation was promoted by both Dems and GOP'ers as it had the blessing of Pres. Bush and Sen.Ted Kennedy (I like the sense of familiarity engendered by "Ted"). Yes, there were so many flaws in that legislation as it moved along that a reform was clearly needed, but instead of passing a new *law*, Common Core has come along as an alternative, not instated by legislation to be reviewed by our representatives with a response from the public, but as a *fait accompli* that has been imposed on the public by a vast strategy implemented by government bureaucrats concentrated in the U.S. Dept. of Education, masters of red tape in educational bureaucracies in our state governments, NGO's (that have a stake in consulting, providing curricula, and analyzing test composition and results), software developers of educational

software, and educational book publishers (often participating in corporate conglomerates with the software developers).[6]

_____

[6] The 1965 Elementary and Secondary Education Act, the first federal attempt to regulate and finance schools, stated: "Nothing in this act" shall authorize any federal official to "mandate, direct, or control" school curriculum. The 1970 General Education Provisions Act stipulates that "no provision of any applicable program shall be construed to authorize any" federal agency or official "to exercise any direction, supervision, or control over the curriculum, program of instruction or selection of instructional materials by any" school system. The 1979 law that created the Department of Education forbids it to exercise "any direction, supervision, or control over the curriculum" or "program of instruction" of any school system. The amended Elementary and Secondary Education Act reiterates that no Education Department funds "may be used . . . to endorse, approve, or sanction any curriculum designed to be used in" grades K-12.

Despite all those emphatic words, Obama's Department of Education, headed by an alumnus of the Chicago Democratic machine and other leftists, seeks to mold the minds of all our children into supporters of big-government. Their vehicle to accomplish this is Common Core, which is artfully designed to impose de facto national uniformity while complying with all those explicit federal prohibitions.

The mechanism of control is the tests that all students must take, which will be written by the people who created Common Core. If students haven't studied a curriculum "aligned" with Common Core, they will have a hard time passing the tests required for a high school diploma and entry into college.

As explained by education researcher and author Darcy Pattison, the Common Core gang in 1996 gathered a cozy group of rich big businessmen, six governors, and a few other politicians and founded an organization called Achieve Inc. Working backward from the 12th grade down to kindergarten, this eventually morphed into the Common Core State Standards. Achieve Inc. started implementation of Common Core with 13 states, but a national curriculum was still the goal, and a congressional debate about that would have been a political risk. So the Common Core advocates bypassed most elected officials and went straight to each state department of education. By 2009, 35 states had endorsed Common Core.

Common Core advocates then announced that "standards" had been developed "in collaboration with teachers, school administrators, and experts . . . to prepare our children for college and the workforce." By 2011, 45 states signed up even though the final draft of the standards was not yet available and they had never been field tested.

Still careful to skirt the laws barring federal control of curriculum, Education Secretary Arne Duncan used federal funds to bait the states to align with Common Core by offering bonus grants from the federally funded Race to the Top program.

The Common Core promoters, whose goal is a national curriculum for all U.S. children despite laws prohibiting the government from requiring it, used the clever device of copyrighting the standards by two non-government organizations, the National Governors Association Center for Best Practices (NGA Center) and the Council of Chief State School Officers (CCSSO). That enables Common Core advocates to force uniform national standards

From compassionate conservatives to left-wing ideologues, we see a flood of rejection of older educational modalities. Every single aspect of earlier education is under fire: blackboards, whiteboards, books, great literature, classrooms managed by teachers, learning in school (many reformers want learning to be mainly at home, on computers, with the work supported by the schools), length of school day, school week, and school year, and length of years in compulsory education, libraries, length and types of homework assignments, school food programs, sex education, student data collection, grading parameters, school security, size of schools, numbers of students in classrooms, testing frequency and content, teacher evaluation, requirements vs. electives, names of departments in high schools, descriptions of teacher qualifications, requirements for tenure and nature of tenure, and eligibility requirements for administrators in terms of

---

while claiming that the laws prohibiting federal control of curriculum are not violated. Those organizations have very official names as though they are government agencies, but they are actually private groups financed by foundations, Bill Gates, and various corporations.

No one may copy or reprint the standards without permission, and states that sign on to Common Core may not change the standards. The license agreement that states must sign in order to use Common Core states: "NGA/CCSSO shall be acknowledged as the sole owners and developers of the Common Core State Standards."
http://www.eagleforum.org/publications/psr/mar14.html

experience, publications, or evidence of specific knowledge (all three criteria are being abandoned). This writer can assure you this is only a partial list of the "reforms" (really, *irreversible changes*) that are being implemented at the moment you are reading these words.

Yet, I would propose these reforms or "irreversible changes" are exercises in futility, and could possibly even lead to the mental and physical enslavement of the population instead of leading to, as DeToqueville envisioned, a thoughtful and responsible democratic citizenry. Even though these changes are meta-changes being embraced by the entire spectrum of political positions, ultimately they have evolved from a leftist-statist-fascistic worldview – a totalitarian impulse if you will. Over the past 20 years there have been incredible irreversible changes in the schools of New York City; yet do we see "progress" and a real leap forward in quality of graduates, real hope and enlightenment of the citizenry, greater competence in the workforce, more skills in our college entrants, more outflowing of compassion based on man's humanity towards his fellow man, or a prayerful humility born by a desire to serve and please a holy and loving God?

My answer to the above question is: hardly. We have seen a small schools movement driven by the Coalition for Essential Schools that has produced little positive good. Comprehensive high schools have been broken up into small, themed academy schools. The stability of the school system has thereby been undermined because millions of people now hold high school diplomas from high schools that no longer exist. These small, themed academy schools because of limited space, limited funding, and fewer students cannot support the electives and numbers of advanced courses that were offered in the comprehensive high schools. Though the comprehensive high schools had many students doing poorly, the more motivated students and those with greater aptitude existed in sufficient numbers to warrant the offering of the more sophisticated educational opportunities. Since there are not enough of these students in the smaller schools, it is not cost effective to offer those courses.

However, it should also be noted that increasingly, especially in New York City, these small themed schools are offering increasing numbers of Advanced Placement courses. These courses end with advanced tests graded on a 1-5 scale, and many schools give credit towards a degree for students getting a 3,4, or 5 (depending on the college or university). Well in these small schools without a pool of motivated or top students, that is, with students who normally would not qualify for admittance to AP courses, those students are being assigned to those courses anyway for the "experience" of taking those courses, because typically they will get a grade of 1 or 2 for their trouble. When I asked one principal, Dr. Belligerence, why so many students were being put in AP and were they not being set up for failure, he replied that it gave them the experience of taking an advanced course. All sense of reality and proportion is being cast aside. They feel more successful according to Dr. Belligerence, and that is enough for them to take a course they can't hope to succeed in. I don't get it.

Thus there is less high end achievement, and on that basis alone one can see the implementation of greater mediocrity and the downgrading or dumbing down of the educational experience. Further, where has whole language teaching of reading taken us? Phonics is making a comeback, but the whole language people and those who implemented their theories (I emphasize that implementation was based more on theory than practice) were wrong. Phonics prepared students across all levels of achievement better than whole language. This has been shown in study after study. Whole language was to promote more self-esteem in the students and more love for reading and appreciation of books by moving away from "techniques" as the phonics methods were perceived. But do we see an upsurge in love for reading? Hardly. The message from the trenches is that children would much prefer to text or read slogans in a computer than read nowadays. The video game has in many cases replaced reading as a modality for "mental growth" (sic) throughout the formative years. What have these reforms done for education?!! When I student taught 50 years ago, there were four students in my tenth grade class in Philadelphia who were unable to write their names (but were in 10th grade – did you get this?....) This writer will tell you that there are still surprising numbers of illiterate and semi-literate students in our schools. Math skills are incredibly low as well in the high schools. At a community college where I taught, I passed a room where first year students were being tutored to multiply fractions, and another who was being taught how to solve for x in a simple equation (in the 9th grade curriculum for NYC high schools).

How has the gradual elimination of cursive writing helped education? How has bilingual education helped communities of students whose native languages are not English? How have theme schools improved the tone and climate of schools where violence, disruption, disinterest, distraction, and disturbance are the hallmarks of education as lived on the ground EVERYDAY? How have suggested topics for answering essay questions in Regents tests helped students in New York State to learn better? How have Document Based Questions on Regents tests done anything except improve the test scores of the students by providing them with answers to the very questions being asked of them? What indeed is being tested by the so-called standardized tests? Who is answering these questions about the questions? How can the public allow an army of paper pushing bureaucrats sitting around state, city, or federal offices determine the goals and educational fate of their children? [The questions in this paragraph are all rhetorical questions.]

The public schools are making guinea pigs of our children. It is amazing to this writer that the outcomes are not even worse than they are – but believe me, the picture is fading fast…an era of educational decline is coming upon us unless we begin to *retrench four decades of reform and get back to some basic ideas, principles, information, and goals that we have lost sight of.* Why are SAT scores so much lower than 50 years ago? The self-satisfied reply that that is because of our success – so many more kids are going to college, so the greater numbers of those achieving and having motivation are taking those tests. Lower scores are a sign to this benighted crew that our education efforts are succeeding. They love to explain every setback and ignorant policy with the phrase "less is more." Lower scores reveal a growth in opportunity. So, even with easier tests, the scores go down. So, even with changed test-taker-friendly ways of scaling the scores on the tests, the scores go down. David Coleman, President of the College Board, has announced that the SATs will eliminate more difficult vocabulary words (the analogies part of the exam was eliminated a few years ago), that the math section would involve more "explaining" of the problems (meaning the right answer will not be as important) and the penalty for guessing will be eliminated. Would it not make sense to then conclude that with more students going to college, the caliber of college students is going down. In NYC, 80% of the students entering the two year community colleges run by the City need remedial reading, writing, and/or math at the time of enrollment. Is there something wrong with this picture?

Again, you dear reader, may be disappointed that I do not have a five point program to give you to fix the problems that are being brought out in these pages. Shortly, I will be making suggestions. Some of the suggestions will make more sense to you than others, but this book is as much a warning as an optimistic rule book for reform. Yes, in regard to education this writer is saying "ROAD OUT, NO

BRIDGE AHEAD. TAKE A DETOUR." **Please begin to assess the extent and nature of the problem(s) we face based on many of the ideas and actualities you read about in these pages.** We need leaders to carry the ball. We don't need any more NGO's like Coalition of Essential Schools or New Visions. We don't need the big leftist education schools like Columbia Teachers' College or the Harvard Grad School of Education to keep churning out their studies telling us how racist, class driven, and uncreative we are as a society. It's a lot of bilge calculated to promote racial division, to drive wedges of resentment among different income levels, and to dilute the knowledge that education is meant to help us attain. We don't need social justice factories and phony leaders like Bill Ayers and his ilk telling students a lot of bilge. I attended one graduation ceremony at an academically excellent school (but it has been going downhill in recent years) and the keynote speaker was Russell Simmons. This pea brain told the graduates that he had never heard about the school, but that in the limousine coming to the graduation he had been briefed and told that it is one of the best academic settings. "So," he said, "that means you are the smart ones." Then he added, "There are a lot of kids your age sitting in the jails today who are there so you could be in the library." Ladies and gentlemen, there are some of you applauding this remark by Mr. Simmons; others of you are shocked and offended, like me.

You see, there are many people who do not believe that being in jail is a choice, or that striving to get ahead in a good high school is a choice. No. They see that in every society there are winners and losers. In order for there to be winners there have to be losers. So "society" has set itself up so that for the students who are winners, there "have to be" other groups of teens who are in jail. There is in Mr. Simmons' mind and in the minds of many, possibly including our President, who believe in this cause and effect. They believe that if there are fewer winners or if you take away from the winners, so-called, we will have fewer losers. The idea of individual choice and individual responsibility are depreciated. The fact that there are tens of millions of students who are not the top students or may be poor students but who, also, are not in jail seems to escape pundits like Mr. Simmons. And there are literally billions of people in the world who are illiterate, poor, sick, and hurting who are not in jail. People do not have to be in jail because others are high achievers. The system does not require it, and the existence of most of the people who are not high achievers and also not in jail proves my point.

It behooves everyone in society to fight this insidious philosophy enunciated by the smug Mr. Simmons because it completely puts the disadvantaged members of our society at a greater disadvantage. Why? The answer is that we all benefit from the gifts that a minority of the population may have. If someone becomes a surgeon, he or she can and will save many lives that would not be saved if that person never became a surgeon. So, for example, if we convert a comprehensive high school to an academy school in a so-called poor neighborhood, there will be fewer opportunities for the gifted minority students, and they will have diminished opportunities to become, for example, surgeons, and this in turn will affect the life spans of people in all strata of society.

Reform of the schools can only come about from the vision of true educators. We have some leaders, albeit very few, who are on the right track: www.eagleforum.org, www.advocatesforacademicfreedom.org, www.constitutionalcoalition.com , www.frc.org , and www.conservativeteachersofamerica.com . We also want to note the writings of E.D. Hirsch, the more recent writings of Diane Ravitch, Paul Horton (http://whatiscommoncore.wordpress.com/2013/04/02/video-chicago-history-teacher-paul-horton-on-common-core-and-corporate-collusion/), and Charlotte Iserbyt (www.deliberatedumbingdown.com). I also do not want to forget Prof. Robert Weissberg whose latest book *Bad Students, Not Bad Schools* provides a tour de force survey of the studies that prove that "reforms" of our schools are largely not working.

We need visionaries and people of impeccable character, integrity, hope, morality, love, and brilliance of mind. I am praying to God every day that true leaders will emerge in our society.

PART ONE:

DOWNWARD SLIDE INTO A PIT OF IGNORANCE, BAD BEHAVIOR, LOSS OF INDIVIDUALITY AND UNFREEDOM

Where We Are; What We Need

Karen Schroeder is already one of the most lucid, positive, morally elevated, and focused education leaders we have.[7] Her influence will undoubtedly grow as the tragically anti-educational reforms of Common Core kick in. I hope that society will be able to pick up the pieces. However, it is unlikely since Common Core is marred from day one by excessive federal involvement, lack of public debate, hundreds of misassumptions about education, and skyrocketing costs. Without federalism (Common Core attacks and decimates state control of education), godly values, promotion of achievement rather than self-esteem (my parents only went through 8th grade, but their self-esteem was intact), and character development, we shall be producing (and have already begun doing so) some of the most

---

[7] The applause of this writer for any individual educator is not meant to imply that said individual would necessarily applaud this writer, nor should an implied endorsement of said writer for this book be assumed. Schroeder's website: www.advocatesforacademicfreedom.org

dumbed down, opinionated, narcissistic people ever seen on the face of the Earth. Further, the educational system is being "gamed," not valued as intrinsically significant, by the majority of students.

I taught in one high school where 75% of the students cut every class more than three times a term, truancy was rampant, and lateness to class by 10-20% of the students was a daily given (20 minutes passing time between classes). The response of the school was to tell teachers to have a lateness book, and have the students sign in when late. Since about 50% of the students were failing each class, do you think that was anything but a joke. Then, adding insult to injury, if any teacher actually failed 50% or more of his/her students, said teacher was called in by the Assistant Principal to explain himself/herself. Actually, for six of my twenty years, I believed that I was part of a criminal conspiracy. Later, I transferred to a top high school where there were many brilliant students, but under pressure from Mayor Bloomberg (NYC) and his minions, the academic quality of the school began to decline, and there was a decline in morale among both students and teachers.

This kind of statement about morale, however, would have no meaning under Bloomberg where knowledge, relationship, and responsibility took second place to systems, statistics, software, and change for change sake. You see, Bloomberg and his minions hoped for the Taylor effect -- remember that study where they found that just making changes increased employee productivity, but the upward curve was only temporary, and in a short time lapsed. So, with the wrong emphases by Bloomberg, just because they were vast changes from traditional education, there was a slight upward blip in gra-duation rates and state exam scores as well as pro-motion rates, but not enough to justify the changes. Now they're slipping back. Also, as Shakespeare would say, here's the rub: achievement levels among minorities slipped precipitously. When I arrived at my prestigious academic high school fully one-third of the students were African-American and another ten percent were Latino. 15 years later the school was only 10-12% African-American with a smattering of Latinos. Likewise, the number of African-Americans admitted to the city's top academic high school, Stuyvesant, dropped to something like 2%.

Watch the present breed of "reformers." It's interesting to note that the liberal and leftist teachers in the New York high schools would agree with most of what I am writing here even though I am a conservative (actually it would be more correct to call me a rational centrist). Why? Because the anti-educational thrust of what is passing for reform today is something these teachers are living with every day. They see the slippage in student commitment, student preparedness, and student achievement. It actually goes beyond even the culture wars of America, and is opening the door to a 'brave new world' where technology is wed to control and the 'big brother' mindset is implemented in a way that even the statists/leftists had not anticipated with their support of big government or socialism. (However, the real hardcore leftists would say that the controls and dehumanization that some on the left might deplore are merely unnecessary vestiges of a bourgeois humanism that needs to be dispensed with.) The new juggernaut of "reform" is clearly going beyond the left-right divide in many ways, although many of those promoting it might have originated or been formed by the Left. The left's ideas are actually being co-opted by superior geniuses of organization who have a vision of control by master puppeteers that is statist but not strictly speaking neo-Marxist or neo-Fascist, but draws on those roots for its *modus operandi*.

Have you noticed that vocational education has almost entirely been eliminated from secondary schools as well as the business track in our urban centers? The three track system – academic,business, and vocational -- at some point was deemed elitist. Didn't every kid deserve a college education? Weren't we pigeon-holing the young and denying them opportunities for college by "tracking" them? And ultimately wasn't there something racist and ignoble about categorizing people who might have legitimate aspirations for college and putting them in some other track? Yet, does anyone appreciate the pain that the individual is put through in the college track when he/she is assigned to studies and aspirations that do not suit his or her nature. Of course, there are people mis-tracked, and we need institutions flexible enough and open enough to allow mobility – yes, upward mobility – at different stages of life; but we need to understand that the pressure for college is not only putting a tremendous potential financial burden on students, but is forcing many students too far out of their comfort zone, and, yes, they are becoming quite uncomfortable, and are hurting with the academic demands being made upon them.

Can you put yourself in the place of a teacher in many or even most of today's high schools and imagine what it is like to have to tell 30+ students to open their notebooks, to take notes, to pay attention, to listen up, to memorize (impossible almost in today's climate), and to reason? (Yes, the nature of reasoning – logic, the syllogism even – has almost vanished from secondary education.) Study of grammar has almost vanished even from so-called top schools. More and more students – even the better students – are not doing their homework assignments on a regular basis. [In 1976, this writer serving as an Instructor at Penn State University spent the first six weeks of freshman English teaching intense grammar review. I cannot but ask myself if this were needed then, what kind of "review" is needed now?] At another point in time, this teacher was teaching about the Vietnam War in an honors class and one student raised his hand and asked me, "Is it true that Vietnamese women would put razors in their vaginas so that American soldiers would have their d---s cut off?" This type of question – whether you deem it to be a smart-aleck question or just a stupid, irrelevant question – would not have been asked even 15 years ago. The tone and nature of classroom dialogue and student participation and levels of understanding have been declining at an accelerated rate.

And what is the response to all this? One response is the Common Core, and another response is to lengthen the school day, the school week, and the school year, even beginning compulsory education at age two. Common Core and extensions of educational control of the individual are sets of ideas that are converging. Remember, that when compulsory education began it was only four months of the year, and did not extend to age 17. It is important that all of us begin connecting the dots between so-called "needed reforms" and the desire to control and semi-enslave the individual. You, dear reader, must begin to connect the dots. That's one of the reasons why this book has been written.

Common Core State Standards (CCSS) is a set of standards developed by state departments of education, educational book and software publishers, and various NGO's (non-governmental organizations), and is coordinated by the Federal government which is setting up national tests for all grades and all subjects taught to assure a type of "quality control" (sic) nationwide. It is important to note that state legislators are not and have not been holding hearings about the progress of the Common Core. Rather, when state officials are involved with Common Core, they are educational bureaucrats connected with the state's department of education or with governmental purchasing offices. Direct feedback from the people has not been and is not being solicited. Laws have not been passed authorizing Common Core in each of the states.

However, the states have vied for "Race to the Top" funds from the Federal government's Department of Education, whereby states that meet certain federal criteria are eligible for the funds. These funds have been the carrot on the stick to attract state commitment to Common Core via each state's governor and education department. So the federal government is funding Common Core and the federal government is creating the tests for Common Core, and has set up the standards to determine whether the states are complying with Common Core standards (yes, you read correctly, there are standards of the standards). Yet, at the same time, because of the Tenth Amendment to the U.S. Constitution, around which the federal government is doing an end-run [the Tenth Amendment reserves to the states all powers not given to the federal government in the Constitution, and education is one of those powers], the federal government is saying that they are not requiring the content for this new national curriculum; hence, control of education still remains with the states as required by the U.S. Constitution.

Many sob stories have been published in newspapers about how the little children are in tears after taking some of the supposedly more difficult Common Core tests given in the early grades. While the concerns about Common Core testing too early are all valid; however, the threat to freedom, both in terms of the threat to federalism (federal encroachment on states) and the threat long-term to kids because of the data collection component of Common Core are ultimately even more important. Common Core requires that 400 questions about each student be answered, and that the answers to these questions and the progress of all student educational data be tracked during the entire time a student is in school – tracked in a federal database created for that purpose.[8]

---

[8] Peter Greene, in a serious vein, explains that the Common Core standards are integrally connected to the collection of data.

They can't be changed or revised–contrary to the nationally and internationally recognized protocol for setting standards–because their purpose is to tag every student and collect data on their performance.

They cannot be decoupled from testing because the testing is the means by which every student is tagged and his/her data are collected for Pearson and the big data storage warehouse monitored by amazon or the U.S. government.

He writes … the Grand Design is– a system in which student progress is mapped down to the atomic level. Atomic level means test by test, assignment by assignment, sentence by sentence, item by item. We want to enter every single thing a student does into the Big Data Bank.

But that will only work if we're all using the same set of tags.

We've been saying that CCSS ("Common Core State Standards") are limited because the standards were written around what can be tested. That's not exactly correct. The standards have been written around what can be tracked.

The standards aren't just about defining what should be taught. They're about cataloging what students have done.

Remember when Facebook introduced emoticons. This was not a public service. Facebook wanted to up its data gathering capabilities by tracking the emotional states of users. But if users just defined their own emotions, the data would be too noisy, too hard to crunch. But if the user had to pick from the Facebook standard set of user emotions– then Facebook would have manageable data.

Ditto for CCSS. If we all just taught to our own local standards, the data noise would be too great. The Data Overlords need us all to be standardized, to be using the same set of tags. That is also why no deviation can be allowed. Okay, we'll let you have 15% over and above the standards. The system can probably tolerate that much noise. But under no circumstances can

Also, for decades, exams, both course exams and standardized exams, followed the development of curricula. *The "standards" were in the courses.* The body of knowledge dictated the kinds of tests and questions on tests. *Now the mindset has changed where the tests are dictating the curricula, and even the methods of teaching.* It is this reversal that is so very wrong!!! As a Harvard University master teacher, with 30+ years of experience, I have studied the educational process in depth, as well as taught for decades at the college and secondary school level (even a few stints in the middle schools). There are no easy answers, but the

---

you change the standards– because that would be changing the national student data tagging system, and THAT we can't tolerate.

This is why the "aligning" process inevitably involves all that marking of standards onto everything we do. It's not instructional. It's not even about accountability.

It's about having us sit and tag every instructional thing we do so that student results can be entered and tracked in the Big Data Bank. And that is why CCSS can never, ever be decoupled from anything. Why would Facebook keep a face tagging system and then forbid users to upload photos?

The Test does not exist to prove that we're following the standards. The standards exist to let us tag the results from the Test. And ultimately, not just the Test, but everything that's done in a classroom. Standards-ready material is material that has already been bagged and tagged for Data Overlord.

The end-game is data-tracking, not standards. And that helps to explain why CCSS was written without consultation with educators; without participation by early childhood educators or those knowledgeable about students with disabilities; why there is no appeals process, no means of revision, why they were written so hurriedly in 2009 and pushed into 45 states and D.C. by Race to the Top. http://dianeravitch.net/2014/03/25/peter-greene-connecting-the-dots-between-ccss-and-big-data/ See also http://www.insidehighered.com/news/2013/01/25/arizona-st-and-knewtons-grand-experiment-adaptive-learning#ixzz2wkgLQ1ZS

Common Core State Standards are not improving anything. They are not state standards; rather, they put testing before curricula when it should be the reverse; they do not have a standard for deciding what an educational standard is or should be, and by being "common" they diminish all that is ennobling in education (for example, replace great literature with government reports to improve literacy - what a sham!). Parents. Educators. Politicians. Keep fighting against this pernicious "reform."

So, in sum, the national or federal government coordinates CCSS, funds CCSS, writes tests for CCSS, and publicizes CCSS, but says it is not dictating content for CCSS. Incredibly, officials across the land, both Republicans and Democrats are buying into this bogus and dangerous progress of events. This CCSS is a threat to every child in this country in terms of his or her ability to think and to participate as a free individual in a free society, a citizen defined by local loyalties and by his or her individuality and not by national priorities far removed from considerations that really do and should bear on the lives of young people growing up in our society.

The cost of implementing this is phenomenal and that cost will include the collection of extensive data on each and every student in America that will follow him and her through college and possibly beyond. Combine this with "school-to-work" concepts in education where the state channels people into certain careers and even particular jobs, and the specter of state socialism or state syndicalism rears its ugly head.[9] The state in the form of the federal government will guide each and every individual to his or her workplace destiny.

Some reforms emphasize "differentiated instruction" where each student goes along at his or her own pace. This might seem kind, but that would be a superficial observation. Since each is going along at his or her own pace, there will be no stigma attached to only being at a 5th grade level. He or she will walk down the aisle with his or her peers. Yet, in reality, it will mean that the attainment of a high school diploma will not only suggest mediocrity as it now does in most cases, but it will have become so diluted as to be meaningless.

---

[9] See my article "The Great Education Power Grab" originally published at www.americanthinker.com, August 14, 2014.

This new differentiated approach will be aided by new technology, and in particular a new software called iZone. The iZone approach shifts education away from the teacher to the computer. The student will be learning from the computer lessons both at home and in a "school" building. The teacher will then assist the computer by grading some of the student's projects or assignments, and answering some questions that the computer may not be able to address (although this software will be increasingly interactive). This will mean less cost overhead for buildings and teachers, and the teachers, who will not be doing the core teaching or developing lesson plans, will need to be less qualified and therefore less expensive than today's teachers. This will reduce the cost of education, and will eliminate relationship as a central part of the learning process (i.e., the relationship between teacher and student(s)).

WHAT ARE YOUR EDUCATIONAL CONCERNS?

What really is wrong with today's schools, particularly urban secondary schools? How can faith, freedom, and family be re-established in education in the USA? Why are kids becoming dumber every year? Are reforms aimed at helping the so-called "underclass" really helping them? Has "politically correct" education become a strait jacket for learning so the search for truth and the upbringing of a thoughtful, responsible citizenry is being overthrown? Is the school supporting the home or is it attempting to supplant the home? (Instead of parents being *in loco parentis*, the parents are now *in loco educationensis [to coin a term].*) Where have we been in urban secondary education, and where are we going? Are we increasingly pathetic despite our software and our algorithms, or are we making progress in knowledge, morality, creativity, analytic and synthetic thinking, caring, the brotherhood of man, and greater motivation and responsibility? Are students demonstrating better character development than in decades past?

This book is rejecting the technocrats, but not technology. We are rejecting secular humanism, Marxism, and Marxism in the guise of progressivism. We are rejecting every attempt to portray the people as being citizens of the world more than being citizens of the USA! We are rejecting spoon-feeding of students. We are rejecting namby-pamby and wishy-washy. We are rejecting a state-driven and controlled education system where the populace from coast-to-coast and beyond the coasts is brought up under rules that drive a greater and greater subservience to the federal government. We reject control of our minds, our health, our careers, our childbearing and child raising, our values, our individual and community goals, our food opportunities, our entertainment, our Internet and TV watching, and our recreation by an all-seeing (supposedly), all-knowing (supposedly), and pervasively controlling federal and state government operating in partnership with vast corporate interests!!!

We are embracing rationality, love of country, family values, noble deeds, heroes of mind, politics, business, literature, and science, kindness and compassion, creativity, morality, responsibility, cleanliness of mind and body, respect for each other and for authority, love of Almighty God, punishment for wrongdoing, logical as well as common sense thinking, and the dignity and worth of every human being. We are embracing Western Civilization. We recognize that the history of the West is primarily a history of a Christianized West embracing the intertwined threads of Hebraic and Greco-Roman ideas, institutions, and ideals. We must recognize our cultural roots not only in the Renaissance and Enlightenment, but in the Protestant Reformation, and before that in Catholic Europe.

PRAY FOR PRAYER

Big city education is against family, faith, and freedom. We all know that prayer was thrown out of the schools in the 1960's.[10] School-initiated silent prayer also is not allowed. The U.S. Senate a few years ago failed to move ahead with a prayer amendment to the U.S. Constitution. That drive was spearheaded by James Dobson to his eternal credit. But there continue to be struggles in the courts over the extent to which student expressions of prayer (that is, student initiated prayer) is lawful at school-wide events like graduations, assemblies, proms, or any other gatherings. Yet, get this, in the New York

---

[10] See footnote 3.

public schools, Kwanzaa can be celebrated under the official aegis of a school's administration. Kwanzaa poses as an African holiday or festival having to do with harvest, but in fact it also includes ancestor worship. However, African-born friends of mine have told me that this holiday was never heard of in Africa. In fact, it was begun by a radical black power leftist in San Francisco.[11]

What about Muslim students? In many schools they are allowed to use assigned room spaces for their daily prayers to Mecca. Nobody says peep. It is a well-kept open secret. They are assigned school space, so it is a school sanctioned use of school property for religious purposes. Separation of church and state suddenly does not apply! Duh!? These are examples of politically correct "applications" where the so-called "wall of separation between church and state" (a phony "wall" introduced in the late 1940's by a liberal member of the Supreme Court) is not consistently enforced.

---

[11] A brief description of Kwanzaa can be found at http://www.africa.upenn.edu/K-12/Kwanzaa_What_16661.html The bio of Dr. Maulana Karenga, the American-born black power advocate who created this event, can be easily found if one googles his name.

PUBLIC EDUCATION ATTACKS
FAMILY VALUES

In New York State, high schoolers can obtain abortions without parental consent. There are many citizens of New York who, although otherwise well-informed, do not know this. Many high schools have "health centers" that refer girl students for abortions. [In New York City, an African-American baby only has a 4 in 10 chance of surviving the womb.] These referrals take place after 10-15 minute interviews. A woman who headed up one of these "clinics" told this writer that it was better for the girls to abort because the babies would be born into the same poor home lives as the students, and they are being "saved" from dysfunctional family situations. The conclusions of the pregnancy counselors would be drawn based on brief interviews with the pregnant ninth, tenth, and eleventh graders. The interviews were made within the context of an ideological framework that already supposed that there was nothing wrong with abortion, that it is a social good, and that females could, would, and should benefit from this "choice." [Can there really be choice without extensive knowledge of the consequences to oneself or others and an appreciation of the values and implications of one's decision?] How can one tell the youth about the importance of education, when society has cavalierly allowed over 50 million persons to go out of existence? The significance of all our human endeavors is dwarfed by this holocaust in our midst.

Further, high schools give out free condoms to students who request them. In NYC, this is often done through a counseling arm of the Guidance Departments, called SPARK. The SPARK counselor deals with issues of teenage sexuality and drug use, whereas the guidance counselors usually respond to behavior problems within the school, and primarily deal with issues related to academic progress. Students voluntarily go to the SPARK counselor for different group sessions dealing with their personal feelings, and the program provides a kind of quasi-therapy. The emphasis is not on abstinence, but on "safe sex." SPARK is the distribution point for condoms in many schools, although sometimes they are made available in other offices.

Abortion is seen as a legitimate option for girls, and is a matter that may come up before actual pregnancies under the heading of "unsafe" sex. If a girl becomes pregnant that means she has engaged in a form of unsafe sex. The sin of premarital sex is now an act of unsafe sex. There is no longer a father with a shotgun or threats to demand that the boy who impregnated the girl marry her. Indeed, the idea of marriage is totally out of the question.

Also, homosexual relations are "accepted." There is nothing perverse, sinful, or immoral about LGBT activities. These are unique expressions of "love" and anyone who objects to these liaisons is merely a homophobe or worse. Their belief is that this approach to homosexuality is "non-judgmental." You see it is considered judgmental, uptight, and the height of unkindness to say that a given behavior is immoral. The idea that sex outside of love and marriage is not an appropriate activity, let alone a SINFUL activity, is foreign and disgusting to SPARK counselors and to the vast majority of guidance persons now in the urban high schools, especially in NYC.

A few years ago, one of the Chancellors of the Dept. of Education (Fernandez by name), a former heroin addict, was promoting an item called "the Rainbow Curriculum." This curriculum attempted to legitimate same sex relations using books about two "daddies" or two "mommies." After a public outcry led by ministers throughout the city and other offended heterosexual citizens, the curriculum was rescinded. The little kids in first, second, and third grades did not have to read about a mommy named Steve. However, within the past year, same sex marriage has been made legal in the state of New York. One can be certain that this curriculum will be reinstated with an even more glowing report to the kids about the joys of same sex coitus. In the past, parents could "opt out" of sex ed for their kids. It's not clear to this writer if this will be permitted in the future now that same sex marriage is legal in New York State.

Another common lesson in health education is on how to put on a condom. Both male and female teachers demonstrate to ninth and tenth graders how one puts this item on a cucumber or a banana. This disgusting promotion of sex to the young was explained one day to this writer in a teachers' cafeteria in a large urban high school. The lady teacher was so proud of this work with all its "progressive" implications. To her mind, she was saving many kids from unwanted pregnancies and all kinds of STDs. Only these assumed protections were in her mind. However, STDs at that time were yearly rising among teens as well as teen pregnancies. Despite this full court press of dependency on condoms, vast numbers of kids were becoming infected with STDs. One might normally conclude that there was more pre-marital sex than ever before in U.S. history. But this did not deter the diehard educators who believe in this type of instruction. To their minds, the epidemic of unwanted pregnancies and diseases would have even been worse without their efforts. "Kids will be kids, y' know," is their standard clichéd thought. The thought that they might be contributing to teenage lust by legitimizing the activity seems far from their minds.

And one thing is for sure: the morality of this student fornication and oral/anal sex never entered their minds. They would not consider the safe sex instruction as encouraging promiscuity. Many of these educators are opposed to promiscuity; yet none is willing to entertain the idea that one, two or three sexual liaisons is "promiscuous." "Out with the old; in with the new" is their subconscious motto. This writer turned to one "progressive" sex education teacher and told her forthrightly that he had one wish for her: namely that she "would lose her funding to teach sex ed." She didn't say hello to me for two years after that comment.

They are analyzing the data like crazy in the schools. That was the method of Mayor Bloomberg, and "data driven education" has caught fire with "reformers" throughout the country. Bloomberg was a master strategist who was gifted in manipulating numbers and pushing numbers to the forefront in public debate. He's a genius in financial organizations having been the head of an investment bank and the head of a financial news service that has earned him billions of dollars. And, **guess what**, surprise (!), financial organizations are all about numbers. But **guess what**? Numbers come into education, but are not as central as they are in finance. Other matters like facts, analysis, synthesis, logical thinking, creativity, persistence, study habits, vision, responsibility, health (mental and physical), values, self-control, and enthusiasm all to the purpose of forming a life (not making a profit only) must be addressed, and **guess what**, they are to be addressed SIMULTANEOUSLY. So I think I could be considered "wholistic," but even here it must be clarified that one man's wholistic vision or concept may not be found in someone else's. "Wholistic" has to do with building the developing youth of society in higher Western, American, Judeo-Christian educational values. I am aware that there are other educators who consider wholeness to be developed by setting some of Shakespeare's plays to rap music. Another teacher I knew who was seen to kiss students on the lips in the hallways obviously had a more touchy-feely version of wholeness in mind.

APLUSNYC.COM GETS A C-MINUS

There is a website with the URL www.aplusnyc.com that is a kind of self-anointed policy hub. My tendency is to call this policy hub a policy humbug, although a few valid points appear. Like the NYC Department of Education (DOE) Disciplinary Code, they write about student mis-behavior in the most general terms. The website is concerned that there are *too many* police in the schools. Having taught in one of three "academy schools" created out of one failing comprehensive high school, this writer can tell you, dear reader, that there were *not enough* police in the schools. There were 18 police in the three schools -- two armed regular police and 16 security personnel (they are part of the NYPD) who were unarmed, but had peace officer status and could arrest students. Frankly, the school was a hotbed of violence and disruption despite that large number! Further, the DOE Disciplinary Code and the aplusnyc.com studies have this in common: they are both very uncomfortable with the idea of punishment. The "P" word incredibly does not appear once in the DOE Code of Discipline. Wake up New York. We need education reform, but not of the pandering variety.

In the www.aplusnyc.com report, the authors are very supportive of something called "social and emotional learning"(SEL). Any educator who hears a phrase like that at a meeting in a high school already knows something bogus is about to be implemented. You see the school as a one stop social service center has taken hold among certain constituencies. The school is more parent than parents. It reminds one of ancient Sparta's ideas where kids are taken away from their families at an early age and are totally raised by the city-state. Tell me frankly (it's a rhetorical question) can any school substitute for the love of a mother and a father? Let me emphasize the word "LOVE." Love includes discipline **and** TLC **and**, hopefully, some measure of wisdom. Frankly I'd rather be raised by a less educated mom and dad with their warts and warps than by teachers (who also have warts and warps) who go home at the end of the day and get a buzz at the local bistro with their friends. They are not there with me (the little kid) while I'm sleeping. They are not there when I'm sick. They're not at picnics with me. Please know that SEL is pure bull!!! Further, the time spent doing it takes away from time spent learning.

Yet, at the same time, kids are coming to school that do not have parents who love and care for them or discipline them. So, then of course the school will develop strategies to instruct those kids in what ordinary decency is. They will be giving them the simplest instruction in the Golden Rule. They will explain (sic) to some children or adolescents that if somebody insults you or writes on your shirt, you are not then to retaliate by knifing that person or slashing them with a razor. Sorry to say, that is the level of "social and emotional learning" we are talking about in most cases. Seeing things in terms of their actual practical realities doesn't sound so lofty I think. The average reader is thinking of some kind of advanced psychotherapy. The reality is that they spend time talking to the wicked ones about the need to control their tempers, and that is all that is really meant. Do I have the answer? No. I don't. But I know that SEL is not an answer. Rather, it's a term for talking-to-death stuff that really must, in all justice, be punished.

No matter what anybody says, the dumbing down of students in NYC is a fact. The misbehavior and criminality is a fact. The hostility to teachers is a fact. The hostility to teachers with 20+ years of seniority is a fact, and more so if they are over 45 years of age. The hostility to book learning is a fact (look at the policy hub for aplusnyc.com...where are the emphases on content or higher order critical thinking?). They are concerned about hostility to art and music as they should be, but what about hostility to history, math, geography, literature, writing, reading, science, rhetoric, grammar, Shakespeare, poetry, essays, short stories? The standardized tests are a cover for lack of learning. The tests are not evaluating learning, but have become *an alternative to learning*. That's the ugly truth. So, the anti-standardized test people are only telling part of the truth. A student can get good grades in the new testing environment so he or she believes he or she has learned a lot and feels smart, but the truth is that their learning is attenuated. It's scary stuff.

The Great Education Power Grab[12]

Did you know that reformers intent on implementing the Core Curriculum (National Standards) have invaded public education? They do not care about kids or about individuals. Armed with statistics and vast software systems, their intent is to establish one-size-fits-all curricula and success parameters in public education nationwide. The scope of their ambitions leads this educator to the conclusion that their underlying impulse is totalitarian.

---

[12] First appeared at www.americanthinker.com May 4, 2013.

These reformers are driving toward the six- or seven-class-a-day high school teaching load, the 9-5 schedule for the schools (or longer), school provided free and compulsory for ages 2 to 22 (or 26), the six- or seven-day school week, and the 12-month school year (with two- or three-week vacation breaks scattered throughout the school year), all controlled by a vast bureaucracy nationwide and justified by the implementation of "national standards." A database of answers to 400 questions by all U.S. students K-20 will be compiled and maintained at a tremendous cost to the public. Forty-six states are already on board. This 20-plus years of control and indoctrination will, if implemented, become a cornerstone of statist control.

Who's doing it? These reforms are led by Bill Ayers, Michelle Rhee, Arne Duncan, and Mayor Mike Bloomberg of New York City. They are also led by educational publishers such as Cengage, Pearson, McGraw Hill, and McDougal Littel. They have a host of supporters including, but not limited to, the Coalition of Essential Schools, New Visions, the Harvard Graduate School of Education, and other NGOs that want to bring equality and progress

[sic] to institutions supposedly failing to their very core. These "reformers" are being abetted by their so-called adversaries, the education unions: UFT, AFT, NEA, and NYSUT. Claiming to object to some of the teacher hostility expressed by the "reformers," these unions actually are 100% in tune with the political and social agenda of those reformers. Why? Because the movement toward "national standards" by these reformers means increased membership and dues for the unions, consolidation of power, and national promotion of their left-wing agenda. The education unions become junior partners in one of the greatest power plays in the history of this country.

The key to their vision, if one can call this Brave New World and 1984 nightmare a "vision," is to bring in a whole new class of school administrators. These administrators do not have teaching experience. Teaching experience tends to breed respect for the individual. Instead, the drive of national standards is to collectivize, to standardize, and to establish one-size-fits-all educational benchmarks, goals, and curricula. The new mandarins of education are people in their twenties or early thirties who are to come in and uproot the supposed garbage of the past. Likewise, pressures are being brought to bear on older teachers and experienced administrators to get out of the way of the "agenda of change."

A few years ago, this writer attended a meeting to recruit teachers into the New York City Department of Education Leadership Academy for prospective principals, and the sophisticated and attractive hostess of the program was asked, "When reviewing applications to the program, do you take into account whether the applicant has written and published any articles of books?" Without hesitation, the woman answered firmly that she does not. Connection with the world of books is not part of leadership in education. On another occasion, this writer even heard one principal in the New York City Department of Education say that he is not interested in having libraries where books just gather a lot of dust; rather, he wants to replace all books with much cheaper and less space-consuming CDs. He added that students do not need literature in high school; they need only skill-sets for proper English usage. Under the Common Core, literature is being de-emphasized in favor of nonfiction, and excerpts will replace the reading of entire texts.

The thrust during Bloomberg's years as mayor of New York City has been to recruit people with little or no experience in education to teach and to run the schools. This supposedly is to refresh a profession that has been too insulated from accountability and new ideas for too long. We saw this in Chicago, when Arne Duncan was the head of the schools. He had only had a little tutoring experience, but his goal was to renovate and revamp the failing system. As far as anyone knows, the system there is still failing.

What, then, do we find? From top to bottom, the NYC Dept. of Education is replete with administrators with little teaching experience. Often selected because they are inexperienced and willing to be as insensitive as a cactus in order to please their superiors, they come to impose themselves as "leaders" on those who are already making great sacrifices as teachers.

Then there are teaching fellows and other "career change" types who have decided they want to begin a new career path in education. They soon learn the realities of life in the schools, and many leave. Many teaching fellows are also brilliant and idealistic, and they come into education to make a difference in the lives of individuals and society as a whole. However, they find that they not only have to deal with incredibly complex and difficult classroom and building situations, but many times are being badgered by clueless administrators who are the "new breed" as described above. This author recently heard a highly regarded principal of a New York City high school say that he considered "classroom management" overestimated in importance. Right. Who needs an attentive, orderly classroom? Let students have a watered down curriculum, let them talk during class, and then give them inflated grades to support their self-esteem. This is to be the new formula for national "progress."

We find people coming into education from facilities management, the petroleum industry, pharmaceutical sales, and lobster wholesaling and delivery backgrounds. This writer has met these people, and the likelihood that they read even one book a year is remote. Are non-readers and non-teachers suited to be educational leaders?

Many, be it for money, security, ideals, or some combination of the above seek administrative positions that they are not ready for. Why aren't they ready? They are not ready because they have not been mentored and inculcated with core educational values that include, but are not limited to, focus on service and on educational values such as curricular innovation, creativity, knowledge, teacher morale, school tone, the family of man, student character-building, and caring/love of all for all (said list can be summed up as "the pursuit of happiness"). The above changes are gradually (and sometimes not so gradually) being implemented in various school districts throughout the country, but national standards (Core Curriculum) are the connecting mechanism whereby the philosophy of education outlined above can be managed at the federal level. The rationale for this is that students in China, Japan, and Singapore regularly do better than U.S. students on international tests of math and science. Therefore, a more comprehensive approach (standards) needs to be taken if we are to remain competitive in the world economy.

Even accepting the highly dubious assumption that we are falling behind those countries, should our schools become as authoritarian as those schools? Are not the Judeo-Christian ideals of love and compassion still valid? Do we want the drones we find in these other cultures. About 46 states have already signed onto "national standards." There is movement in that direction. There are not many articles in the conservative media and blogs challenging this direction. Nevertheless, the danger to culture, to rationality (substituting what to think for how to think), to individuality, and to the tried and true is palpable.

My question to the reader: Do you want American public education to become even more of an ideological monolith than it is at present?

PART TWO: WOULD YOU ENROLL YOUR CHILD IN HELLHOLE H.S.?

A LIVING ALLEGORY: DID THIS STUFF REALLY HAPPEN? YOU BET!

My first fulltime teaching assignment in New York City was at Hellhole High School in the middle of a neighborhood known for poverty, drugs, broken families, and crime. I had been hired after a 2-1/2 hour interview with the head of the Social Studies Department, Dr. Experience, and his assistant, a thirty year veteran, Mrs. Allknowing. After 1-1/2 years of teaching in the school (more about that 1-1/2 years will come later in this book), the school was declared a failing high school by the NY State Department of *Edumacation* (!), and the decision was made to break-up the school into three smaller schools.

The school was certainly a failing school. Only 25% were passing the NY State Regents Standardized Examinations in Social Studies, and an even lower percentage was passing in math and science. Violence and mayhem were always present in the school – fights were breaking out throughout the school all day long, students were being slashed by razor blades and box cutters in the hallways during the passing between classes, cursing was the verbal norm, sex acts were being accomplished in the stairwells and classroom closets, the walls were being defaced with graffiti, toilet seats had been set on fire three times in the girls' bathrooms (Dr. Experience had climbed onto toilet seats in adjoining stalls to use fire extinguishers to put out the fires), teachers were cursing out students and vice-versa, and it seemed that 18 security guards and two full-time armed New York police officers were not enough to begin to restore order.

Among the most disorderly freshman classes, only about 15 minutes of instruction could take place during one class period as it took so long for them to "settle down" and the students would become "restless" again 10-15 minutes before the end of the period. In other classes, one might expect at least 30 minutes of instruction as it took at least 15 minutes for hallways to clear between classes.

Even during the 30 minutes, one could expect constant interruptions with students arriving late, students leaving their seats to go talk to friends on the other side of the room, manicuring of nails, a lot of general talking and hubbub, and heckling of the teacher. I am thinking of one student I had who came to class everyday with an open wash cloth on his head who sat with a malicious grin on his face as if he were waiting to devour his prey. With all of the above experiences, you may be surprised to hear that I was told I by one of the Assistant Principals that I was one of the most effective class managers in the school!

On my first day at Hellhole High, I was ushered into my first class by the principal, the assistant principal of social studies, and seven security guards. The principal spoke to the 9th grade class which was sitting quietly. He said, "Mr. Ludwig will be your new teacher. He is an excellent teacher, and will be here for the rest of the term unlike the other three teachers you had who left. You should act properly towards him and give him your full attention and work hard. Are there any questions?" There were no questions so the principal along with his entire security retinue turned and walked out the door leaving me alone with the class.

Bedlam broke loose. Students started talking loudly, cursing, and two or three chairs were overturned. One kid said "We're goin' to kick your f------- a--." Siri stood up in the back of the room and declared "We got rid of the other three teachers, and we'll get rid of you too!" I had quit an administrative assistant job in a plush office on the 62nd floor or the World Trade Center to be there. I had been working with courteous people and with engineers who knew what they were doing. At lunchtime I could eat in a spacious, well lit, and well stocked cafeteria, and I could go pray with my Christian friends in the Port Evangelistic Association of Christian Employees. Now I was looking into their petulant faces filled with malice and contempt for their teacher. They portrayed me as their enemy, and asserted that I would be defeated.

Can I ever forget the day I had a confrontation with Anthony? I was beginning the class meeting, and Anthony was chasing a girl around the room. She was shrieking delightedly, but moving fast to evade his grasp. I clapped my hands. The bell had rung. "O.k. Anthony, Jeannette, time to begin the class. I want to get started....." Anthony and Jeannette just kept running. Finally, Jeannette slid into her seat, but Anthony came up beside her panting and laughing excitedly as she in a smiling, flirtatious way tried to shoo him away. "Ok, Anthony, you can talk to Jeannette later, why don't you take your seat now so the lesson can begin?" Anthony cast me a malevolent look and grudgingly sauntered back to his seat. As soon as he sat down, though, he began scratching at the veneer that was glued to the top of the wooden desk. With his fingernails, he began ripping off little pieces of his desk top with the expression on his face growing more angry and fierce every second. "Anthony," I spoke to him, "stop tearing up your desk. It's time to pay attention. This is school; you can't spend the time chasing Jeannette. We're here – you're here – to study history. You must understand that." Seeming not to have heard a word I said, his nails continued to attack the veneer finish of the desk. "Anthony, c'mon, I'm not kidding around. You've got to pull yourself together. You're taking this too far. O.k. O.k. I want to talk to you for a minute in the hallway." Anthony got up from his desk with an intense expression of anger on his face, and followed me into the hallway. "Anthony, you don't have to be this way," I said. "You can just decide that you are not going to continue being angry that you can't chase Jeannette anymore. Just say to yourself 'What the heck, I'm here to learn,' and just stop tearing up your desk, take out your notebook and settle down. You can decide to do this…." He looked at me with intense hatred. I sent him back to his seat. But as soon as he sat down, he gave me my answer – he again began tearing feverishly at the top of his desk. It was horrible to see this mania in action. Nothing more could be said. In order to have some semblance of a lesson in the time remaining, I called school security that came and removed him from the classroom.

Students destroyed computers that were provided for their benefit. Mr. Cassanova had worked nights and weekends to find computers and donors of software to set up a computer lab in the school for social studies. He and his cousin sneaked into the school on nights and weekends to do the needed wiring since the school was not, at that time, budgeted for this equipment. For him, it was a labor of love. Yet, the students who used the lab would put glue in the keyboards or in the mice. The simplified programs that were used were still too complex for them, and their short attention spans took forever to do the simply designed work. I mildly suggested to one girl that she move her cursor to a certain spot on the screen and click. Out of the blue, she immediately began cursing me, and ran out of the room and slammed the door.

In another class, one girl walked to a window, opened it wider than the 6" officially allowed, and just as I spoke to her about lowering the window, she jumped out! Fortunately we were on the first floor, but it still was an eight foot drop. Fortunately she wasn't hurt, and told me two years later that she had been high from smoking reefers in the girls' bathroom. Two years later, I was recruiting students for a program the Department of Miseducation had with the Department of Aging, and when I interviewed this same girl, I told her that only students who were "at risk," that is, who had serious problems could join the program, and I added that I was not sure that she had serious enough problems to be in my program. "Mr. Ludwig," she replied, "I'm 19 years old and I'm in 10th grade, so I think I qualify as having 'serious problems'." I signed her up without further ado. Under that program, if students showed up for school in the a.m., they were assigned to intern at a senior center during the p.m. This opportunity could eventually lead to employment in the same facility when they left high school. Also, it was an incentive for certain troubled students to attend their classes for at least a half day instead of being truant for the whole day. This young lady, Tawana, was assigned to a center and doing well. As the reader can already see, she had a good sense of humor despite her bad habits and temper. However, one day, she got into a fist fight with the security guard of the senior center, and was kicked out of the program. Soon thereafter, she dropped out of school, and I never saw or heard from her again.

Hellhole High School was a school with about 2700 students officially on role. However, there was a high truancy rate, and that number typically was not in the school on any given day. In fact, in my classes, about 50% of the students cut 10 times a term, and 75% cut at least three times a term. However, the decision was made to break the school up into three academy schools (small high schools) with about 675 students in each school.

The teachers were asked to choose in order of preference which of the three schools they would prefer to teach in. One school would emphasize humanities, another business, and a third science and math. We were told which of the administrators of the larger school would be principal of each of the three schools. As years passed, under Mayor Bloomberg, teachers would not automatically get their choice of school, but would have to reapply to teach in the three schools, and if not selected would become part of a pool of teachers called ATRs, who would not have a permanent position, but would still be on the Department of Education payroll. Since, at the time of Hellhole High School's downsizing, fewer teachers were needed for the three high schools than for the comprehensive high school, teachers were also given the opportunity to transfer to other comprehensive high schools where there were openings. Thus, every teacher was placed, either in one of the three new schools or in another high school in NYC. No non-teaching teachers were to be retained and paid as would later be the case under the brilliant but strange Mayor Bloomberg.

We were told we could transfer anywhere there was an opening, but this proved to be false. In August, prior to the beginning of the next school year, we were called to a special transfer meeting where we could apply to other schools. Teachers from other schools that had been broken up were also at that big meeting. Each of us received a number at 9:00 a.m. and was told that if our number was called and we did not come forward, even if we were in the bathroom, or had gone out to buy a sandwich, we would lose our place in line, and would have to go to the back of the line.

Eleven hours later, at 8:00 p.m., my number was finally called. I went forward to the front desk manned by Mr. Bureaucrat and his three associates. "Where would you like to transfer Eddie [that's my first name]," he asked as if we were close friends. I then named the top academic high school in the city, Stuyvesant High School, and he and his associates laughed uproariously. "That's impossible Eddie," he retorted, "who ever told you that you could transfer to such a top school with such low seniority?" "Mrs. Getyourrights," I answered, "she said that irrespective of our seniority we could apply to any high school where there was an opening and transfer in, that we would get first preference because our school was having a forced closing." With that, Mr. Bureaucrat and his associates burst into even heartier and more contemptuous laughter. "Eddie, …Eddie…," he said, "that's impossible; there's no way that someone with as little seniority as you have can go teach in Stuyvesant."

"Then how about sending me to a *bad* high school?" I replied. "Hellhole High School isn't even a high school: it's one-third a school, one-third a jail, and one-third an insane asylum…so, if I can't get Stuyvesant, I want to go to a high school, even a bad one…." Again, he and his associates laughed in derision. My palpable pain did not move them in the least. "Eddie," he said, "you will be staying on at one of the three new schools at Hellhole, that's final." With those words, he stamped my paper, "NO TRANSFER," and handed it to me.

I almost collapsed. I asked a colleague of mine to hail me a taxi, and lend me ten dollars to take the car instead of the subway. The next morning I had a temperature of 103, and the day after that I had rashes all over my body, and had to be admitted to the hospital with adult chicken pox. I was quarantined, but a kindly Israeli doctor advised me not to feel like an outcast even though I was quarantined. I was still part of the human race. No transfer from Hellhole, and quarantined with a potentially deadly disease. It was not a high point of my life.

Under the "NO TRANSFER" edict that was stamped onto my paper was another statement assigning me to the new humanities academy that was one of the replacement schools for Hellhole. It had been my last choice of the three schools as I knew the Principal, Mrs. Newthoughts, was someone with a bizarre, radical educational philosophy. Once, as we passed a noisy and unfocused classroom, she said to me, "Hear that, Mr. Ludwig ,…that's the sound of learning." The idea of the traditional classroom where students had to pay attention was considered by her to be out-of-date. Instead, she preferred that all classes be structured around group activities (now called "cooperative learning" as opposed, one may guess, to traditional "competitive learning"), and the groups would be oriented towards "discovery learning." Instead of studying the laws of physics in a textbook and trying to solve problems, for example, students would engage in ingenious group activities by which they might learn the essence of such otherwise abstruse formulae like Force = Mass X Acceleration. The classroom is a place where students discover their subjects' truths for themselves instead of learning them from a textbook or teacher presentation. We were told that blackboards or greenboards at the front and on the sides of the rooms' walls were to be used as little as possible.

At a small meeting we teachers had with her, on one occasion, I suggested that the discovery method was inefficient considering the vast body of knowledge that constituted each of the high school subjects. My point was that even if students could learn some physics by "discovery" it would be the equivalent of reinventing the wheel, since the truths or laws of physics have been discovered and mul-tiplied over the centuries. At best, even assuming that clever lessons were devised whereby these laws and descriptions of physical phenomena could be flushed out, there was not enough classroom time to flush out all the fine points or subtleties of these laws; nor was there time to cover the breadth of material covered in a typical textbook, even an easier textbook.

I told her and the other teachers there that when I studied physics in high school, it was a more traditional way. I was a good student, but could never solve the five star (hardest) problems in the textbook. All I could solve were the four star problems, and frequently I would go to my friend Steve and ask him the key to solving the five star problem. Steve was willing to oblige and would show me what to do, and every time his solution was so simple and obvious that I would ask myself how I could not have seen how to proceed. Yet, even knowing that Steve would show me a simple and clear approach, I still could not solve those five star problems. "Why not?" I had asked myself. And the answer simply was that Steve was better at physics than I.

When I finished relating this anecdote, Mrs. Newthoughts, said, "No, Mr. Ludwig, Steve was not any smarter at physics than you. If you both had been taught using cooperative learning and dis-covery, you would have been able to solve the same problems as Steve, and you would not have formed this misconception about your abilities." What?! Was I hearing her correctly? I went to a top high school, and now she was saying I had been mis-educated. I held degrees from two top Ivy League universities. I had studied at the University of London; yet, I had been miseducated? How could this be?

Yet, two or three months after the above exchange, Mrs. Newthoughts invited me to a workshop for principals, assistant principals, and a few invited teachers – 70 in all – to study about group learning and discovery. We were all seated at separate tables, about 8 at a table. The workshop leader opened the workshop by giving us a problem to solve about pouring a certain amount of water into two beakers. Our challenge was to fill the beakers with a certain amount of water, and to do it in the fewest possible steps. Although I was a social studies teacher, my old love for math came rushing back into my chest and my mind, and I immediately tackled the problem with a lot of fervor. I was working feverishly, and the others at the table just stopped to watch. After five minutes, I had completed the problem in four steps and raised my hand to notify the leader. Two minutes later an Assistant Principal of math from another high school raised her hand, then she ran over to see my answer. She had the same answer, but had taken seven steps to get there.

What happened? Under the method of group learning my group 'won' the competition. We all got credit for knowing. Now I finally understood what Mrs. Newthoughts meant about Steve and me in high school. If he and I were in a group, he still would have been the only one to solve the problem, but I and the other members of the group would have gotten *credit* for solving the problem. Steve would still have been the only one to actually solve the five star problem, but the rest of us would have had that knowledge *attributed* to us. The set-up would not have allowed Steve to stand above the rest of us as he would be forced to "share" his gift with the rest of us. Steve would have solved the problem, but we would not have had to acknowledge Steve was smarter. We would presumably have more "self esteem." Is this not a type of communist or Marxist thinking translated into pedagogical methodology? Teachers in high schools always had done group work from time to time, but this new ideology of group work derived from Marxist social concepts was something entirely new. Did I not know that the political statements of Mussolini and Hitler explicitly rejected individualism (formerly called "liberal individualism" but now called by many progressives "right wing individualism") in favor of statist values, the same as the Marxists in the USSR and other countries? Knowing my history, how could I buy into this misguided pedagogy? I never resented Steve one bit for knowing something I didn't know; I had had no need to be coddled into thinking that he and I were really on the same level. We were equal enough in that we were both 16 year old boys trying to catch a vision of our futures. We shared the everyday life of the school. Why would I want to get credit for physics problems I had not solved?

The first principal who hired me was named Nelson Deceit. At the time I came on board, teachers who "had an appointment" were hired for five years. I was scheduled to come into the school in March, an unusual start time. However, four teachers had been run out of the school by the students since February, the actual start of the term. Dr. Experience had assured me that Mr. Deceit had told him that a five year appointment letter would be forthcoming, so I resigned from my good job in the World Trade Center (O Lord, it's been turned to dust!) and began work. Once I began, Mr. Deceit informed Dr. Experience that the Board of Education would not issue an appointment letter in March, but assured me through Dr. Experience that he would write me a letter in June to guarantee my appointment on a five year basis to the school and the school system. Of course, June came and went, and there was no letter. Finally in August, a week before the next school year began, Mr. Deceit told me to come to his home to pick up the letter. When I arrived, two of the assistant principals were in his dining room studying the computer screen and preparing for the coming school year. Then Mr. Deceit went to his computer, and printed out a letter -- one sentence – stating that I should be appointed to the school system and be retained at that high school. It was five months and two big lies later, and what did I get: a one sentence "letter."

Mr. Deceit was a pathological liar. Yet the teachers would only shrug when this "character trait" came up in conversations. "That's how Nelson is…." Mr. Deceit told the teachers that asbestos was not polluting the air in the school. He said he had received a report from the Occupational Health and Safety Administration that had tested the air quality in the school after some of the old walls in the basement had been opened during a school construction project. It was a building constructed during the 1930's and asbestos was, at that time, used as a standard material in wall and ceiling construction as it is so strongly fire resistant. Over the years, scientists discovered that when asbestos in walls or ceilings is disturbed, it will pollute the air of the building, and, if breathed in on a daily basis, is a carcinogenic agent. Mr. Deceit stated flatly to the teachers that the halls of our building were SAFE.

Yet, as if by divine appointment, the leader of the teachers in the school discovered the results of the air testing lying carelessly on a table in one of the conference rooms. The report – the official report – made it abundantly clear that the air in the school was indeed polluted and being polluted more and more every day. Have you ever read the play "Enemy of the People" by Henrik Ibsen? Wow. The theme is that the health spa that is a small city's main moneymaker and attraction has polluted water. The very place that is central to their economy and known for its health-giving properties is actually a health hazard. To reveal this truth would destroy the economy of the city; yet, to reveal the truth would keep countless numbers of people from becoming sick, or even dying. Thus, Mr. Deceit had again suppressed the truth; only that truth was finally in black and white for all to read! The teachers then, at the beginning of the school year, upon learning of the truth from Mr. Wiseman, refused to begin teaching until the building underwent asbestos removal to protect ourselves and the students from contamination. Mr. Deceit never uttered one word of apology for the false report he had made to us. He shrugged, and the teachers were so obliging that no one even tried to get the Board of Education to ask for his resignation. I was amazed as a new teacher that he had kept his job despite this mendacious effrontery; but the teachers understood better than I that the system was based on collusion and cover-up.

On another occasion, there was a full-scale riot at the school between the Jamaican and the Haitian students. Rocks were thrown. Windows were smashed open. Tools lying around because of construction on school grounds were also thrown or used as weapons. By noon, helmeted riot police and helmeted police on horses were called onto the school campus to suppress the rioting. The school day ended at 12:15, and I made for one of the rear exits of the building, and managed to get home unscathed. Incredibly, at a faculty meeting two days later, Mr. Deceit proudly told the faculty how he had gone to the police station to beg for leniency for the six students who were arrested. He had remained there for over six hours arguing with the police to release the students and expunge their arrests from the police records. Mr. Deceit was so happy to tell us that his tenacity succeeded, and that the male-factors who were central players in all the de-structive mayhem were allowed to leave, and were not charged. To me, this was a case of Tiananmen Square-in-reverse.

As you, dear reader, may recall there were riots by Chinese students in Beijing to demand greater freedoms under the ever-repressive and sanctimonious, power mad government of the

Peoples' Republic of China, and hundreds of those students, the precious, gifted young scholars of the PRC were murdered in the streets. There is a famous photo of one brave young soul standing by himself in front of a tank, and the tank turning around. Well, Mr. Deceit's strategy could be called Tiananmen Square-in-reverse. The former incident was a model of repression. Mr. Deceit's strategy was that of condoning terrible, destructive anarchy, and leaving the leaders and participants with the totally wrongheaded understanding that what they did was still within the tolerable range for citizens. Isn't it clear that Mr. Deceit's ethos was an expression of that extreme permissive ideology in childrearing and citizenship that has been a by-product of the Dr. Spock philosophy of childrearing? Isn't it clear that the attitudes he showed explain why there are more police in the schools than ever in our history; yet, there are at the same time a growing number of violent incidents in the schools? Even when the police do their job and protect people and property from violence, there are those who are at once saccharine and authoritative who will persist with their insisting, their nagging, their awful and self-serving cries about not wanting these poor kids to have felonies on their records! And isn't Mr. Deceit one of a small army of people in charge of our schools, our cities, our government at all levels who, when there is an incident of violence, sexual attack, or robbery in the schools – especially in a classroom – who will blame the teacher rather than those who committed the attack? The teacher may come in with a black eye and a cut, but the principal will ask, "What did you do to provoke this student?"

I personally know of a case where a teacher was merely standing alongside two students who started brawling, and in a split second, one punch thrown by a student caught him in the left eye. The teacher, as required, filed an incident report, and a letter of reprimand was put in his personnel file for being there when the fight started. He was to blame because his eye was in front of the student's fist!

Once, this writer was substituting in a junior high school, and in a particularly wild class, I asserted myself, and confiscated two armloads of weapons from the students – including sticks, pipes, parts of chairs, and chains. I brought the huge pile down to the office of the principal of the school, and told him that the huge load of items had been confiscated from my fifth period class. He asked me to put the items down on top of his file cabinet, and then asked for the names of the students from whom I had taken the weapons. I told him that I was unable to get their names. It was the first time I had ever been in the room or met them, and they would not even give me their names even when I tried to take attendance. The principal, nicknamed Mr. Frankenstein by the teachers, said, "Without their names, there is nothing I can do about it." On another occasion, he made a visit to the same class, and said to me, "This class is out of control." I replied, "Yes, sir, I must agree; since you are the principal, I'm sure you can bring them back to order." He immediately left the room.

Mr. Deceit's permissiveness could be seen in his day-to-day relations with the students as well as in the bigger riot event. On one occasion, I observed Mr. Deceit walking down the corridor on the first floor accompanied by a student who, as they walked, was cursing out the principal at the top of his lungs. The principal kept walking and said to the student, "You'll have to walk faster as I am late for a meeting and don't have time to talk right now." On another occasion, I intervened when I saw one boy chasing another boy around the hallway and in and out of classrooms with an open pen knife. The student with the open knife gave me the weapon but kept protesting that he was "only playing."

As was the student m.o. when confronted by authority in the school, they would keep talking non-stop protesting their innocence and righteousness, and, as I walked with him to the principal's office, I kept putting my fingers to my lips to indicating that he should stop mouthing off. Sometimes I would say, "Stop talking." Suddenly, Mr. Deceit appeared, and I told him about the incident with the knife. Instead of the principal beginning disciplinary action leading to suspension and a parent conference, the principal looked at the boy and said, "I suppose he said he was only playing." Then, addressing the boy, he said, "Why are you sitting so quietly? Why don't you explain yourself to Mr. Ludwig and tell him why you were chasing the other guy?" I was stunned. Incredulous. Another victory for do-nothingism. Another victory for irresponsibility. Another victory for the bad over the good. Mr.

Deceit who looked bespectacled, wise, and sincere (like the father of Dennis the Menace) was another so-called educator who despised uprightness of purpose.

The school had many large, dark stairwells. One day as I stepped through the exit doors into one of the stairwells, I heard a voice saying, "Mr. Ludwig, I love you." Being of a mystical bent, I wondered if this were the voice of an angel calling to me from the supernatural ether. I looked around and saw no one, but the voice repeated the same refrain. "Who are you? Where are you?" I asked. "Up here," the voice said, drawing me to look upwards towards the dark space at the top of the flight of stairs up to the next floor. "I really like your classes – you're so clear, and you tell a lot of good jokes; I really learn in your class." I was delighted to hear these complimentary words. "Who is it?" I asked. "Tyrone," the voice answered, "Tyrone Smith from fourth period." "Tyrone, yes Tyrone," I replied into the shadow-filled staircase. "Thanks a lot for the good words Tyrone," I replied. "I'm glad you feel like you're getting a lot out of my class; but I just have one question for you." "Yes, Mr. Ludwig, what's that?" he responded. "Well, Tyrone, my question is: if you like my class so much, why don't you ever come?"

Mrs. Newthoughts sent a letter to Mr. Schwartz criticizing his teaching. Mr. Schwartz was old, overweight, and walked with a cane. His long white hair was often matted and he looked somewhat unkempt. He was a teacher from another era marked not only by his infirmities but by the fact that he loved to learn, and I would venture to say, knew right from wrong. He pulled me aside outside the principal's office at the end of the school day on a Tuesday. "What do you think of this?" he asked, showing me the letter he had just received from Mrs. Newthoughts through her secretary. I read the sharply worded and angry missive quickly, and looked at Mr. Schwartz. "She hates your guts," I said. "That's what I thought too," he replied. We looked into each other's eyes incredulous that such a damning letter had been written. Vitriol and hatred seemed to emanate from the page on which it was typed. It was a visceral, personal criticism from the principal. It expressed not only criticisms but an abiding hatred and contempt for the man. He was being considered dirt beneath her feet. His decades of service did not even partially offset the deficiencies she perceived in his teaching. Two weeks before in front of me she had commanded him to get up on a chair to decorate his classroom even though he was overweight and could hardly walk across the room.

All I could bring myself to say was, "I'm sorry Mr. Schwartz." We looked into each other's eyes for the last time. The next morning he took a car service to school, paid his fare, walked the twenty feet across the sidewalk to the side doors of the school, stepped up one step onto the ledge in front of the doors, and passed out on that ledge and died before the medics could even arrive.

The following day, Mrs. Newthoughts arranged a school assembly to memorialize Mr. Schwartz, but in the hallway told another principal supervising in our complex of schools that "it's good he died because it saved me the trouble of getting rid of him."

Most of the students in the high school in a so-called disadvantaged neighborhood spent the entire class time talking, doing their nails, calling across the room, singing, squirming in their seats, or "wrestling" with questions that could have been answered by a sixth grader in a more normal setting. If a teacher in that school failed 50% or more, that teacher was called in and told they must be doing something wrong if so many failed, and if the supervisor were told that of that 50%, one-half had not attended class more than three times in the report period or term, the teacher was told that that must be because his or her class was uninteresting and poorly taught. One consultant at a workshop said that it really was our duty to call our students at home and wake them up if they regularly missed our first, second, or third period classes. One year, three days before graduation, 33 were scheduled to graduate (out of a school that supposedly enrolled 650), but on the day of graduation 56 graduated. The grades were changed in a wholesale fashion on student transcripts so that they could increase the graduation numbers for the school. I saw one boy walk down the aisle with his mortarboard who had only attended two class meetings of my economics class which was one of eight required courses in social studies that students had to pass to graduate.

Everyday was a challenge to meet distracting, disruptive behavior. The first day of classes for one Spring term, the students entered the room, and one student, instead of sitting at a desk, sat down on the floor with his back against the left wall of the room. I asked him to please take a seat, but he didn't say a word and didn't move. He simply grinned de-lightedly. The students entered the room and said out loud, "Why is he sitting on the floor?" I replied to the students that when someone is in a lot of pain they sometimes sit or lie on the floor -- "He's in a lot of pain, but don't worry, I think he'll start to feel better soon, and sit at a desk." I began the class by welcoming the students to the new term, and was happy to see that after 15 minutes had passed, the student gathered himself off the floor and sat at a desk.

Another student refused to leave the room so she could continue her conversation with a girlfriend who was in my class. I asked her, "How many doughnuts are in a dozen?" She thought for a moment, and answered, "Twelve." "Correct," I said, "now you really have to leave because you're too smart to be in this class." She laughed and forthwith left the room

Another teacher from Africa was a strict math teacher. One of the girls in a class came in late to class dressed in scanty clothes, and took a long time to take her seat. Once seated, she began to flirt non-stop with all the boys in the vicinity of her desk, and did not hesitate to talk loudly while the teacher was explaining some aspect of mathematics. The teacher told her to leave the room, and she delightedly took a long time to move from her desk to the door all the while flirting and talking with the boys in the room. As she opened the door to leave, the teacher said to her, "You think you're cute don't you?...." With that she exited the room. However, later the teacher was called to the principal's office as the girl had filed a complaint that he had "sexually harassed" her [sic].

The same teacher had a confrontation with another student on a different day, and while he was arguing with the student, a second student threw a spitball at him. The spitball landed on one of his lips and stuck to the lip. Then, in order to get the spitball off, he spit it off his lip. The student who had thrown the spitball then rushed out of the room claiming loudly that the teacher, Mr. Afrocentric, had spit at him and shouted that his face was "covered with Mr. A's lunger." After these incidents, Mr. A. was removed from the classroom for two years before being acquitted of all charges by an impartial arbitrator. Fortunately, he had a statement from a security officer who was in the hall when the spitball malefactor rushed out of the room to the boy's room, and was able to report that he had no saliva on his face as claimed.

This writer had cafeteria duty in the same school as Mr. A.'s incident, and while standing to the side watching the daily mayhem, one 15 year old girl walked to within 6 feet of where I was standing accompanied by her girlfriend. "That's the one," she said. "He's the one who hit me." I had never seen this girl before in my life, and because of the strict rules against touching, pushing, hitting, or poking any student would never allow myself the luxury of doing any of those things. "What?!" I was shocked and stymied. "What did you say?" I asked. "I've never even seen you before, not once, in my entire life. What are you talking about? I never hit you. Take that back." She looked at me with such a malicious little gleam in her eye, and said nothing. Then she and her girlfriend walked away, and I heard nothing further about her vicious claim.

Another student appeared in one of my classes as a transfer from another high school. He claimed that he had to transfer in because a gang leader at his old high school felt jealous of his interest in the gang leader's girlfriend. His life was being threatened, so he was transferred out as a safety precaution. His version of events remained suspect in my thinking because I learned that he was transferred into his previous high school from the borough's top high school for having a concealed weapon on his person. In short, even before he was the one who was threatened, he had a history of violent behavior.

This student, Luke, was a good looking, very bright student with an athletic build, about 225 pounds. Assignments for classwork that took the other students 1/2 hour to complete, he would complete correctly in about 5-8 minutes. In fact, at his first high school, he had won the freshman poetry prize before he was expelled. I had the idea of mentoring him as he seemed to gravitate towards me and was relatively open in speaking with me. He told me that his home life was a battleground with his parents, especially his mother, and that he usually ended their arguments by cursing her out and walking out of the apartment. I asked him if it weren't possible for him to just decide to be reconciled with his mom. "Can't you just go in one day and tell her that she makes the best spaghetti in New York" I asked. "No," he replied, "I can't." "But," I asked, "God forbid, what if something should happen to your mom? You would have a burden of guilt with you for a long time, or the rest of your life wouldn't you?" He just shrugged and said, "I can't." Incredibly, two weeks later, his mother had a heart attack even though she was only in her forties, and passed from this mortal coil. About two months later, Luke disappeared from school, and was gone for about three weeks. When he returned to school, he gave me a large yellow form – his excuse for his absence. It said that he had been held in Rikers Island, the New York City jail, for that entire time. "What were you in for?" I asked. He had a big smile on his face, and replied, "I was chasing after my father with a knife to stab him." I could hardly believe my ears. "Luke, I don't see why you're smiling about this," I said. "Didn't you ever hear about the Ten Commandments where it says 'you shall honor your father and your mother'?" He just kept smiling, took the signed paper back from me, and left the room.

One day I opened the door to the Men Teachers' Bathroom, and a girl student was zipping up her jeans. "How did you get in here?" I asked. "A teacher let me in," she answered.

Another day at a different high school, I opened a door to a stairwell, and found a girl student giving oral sex to a boy student while another one was watching. But, in a split second, seeing me, she was able to stop, ran down the stairs, and the boy, having stuffed his private parts back in his pants – along with his friend – were down the stairs too.

Another student at Hellhole, Langston, brought two papers as explanation for his absence from my classes. One was a court appearance ticket for assault and robbery in New Jersey, and the other was from a court in New York City for assault. Langston, during the winter months, loved to sometimes adjust my scarf...just a little bit too tight….

During my first term in Hellhole High, my Assistant Principal, in an act of mercy and in order to keep me from leaving the school in disgust, offered to remove two students of my choice from my misbehaved class. This was a rare and generous offer at HH, and I was most grateful. I chose two students – Kenya and Falima – who had been harassing me during seventh period since the day I arrived. The day after I made my choice, they received the green slip notifying them of their change to a different section. But they refused to go insisting that they "really like your class Mr. Ludwig." I asked them, "How do you act when you don't like a teacher?" but they didn't answer. So, they came to the class every day for the next four days, and every day I would have to argue with them and insist that they leave, and threaten to call security before they would leave. Finally, they stopped coming to my class, leaving me with about 7-10 others who were determined to get me through the revolving door (it was March but I was already their fourth teacher since February). Later, when Falima was a senior, she told me that she and Kenya were high all the time, and that that was why they were so uncooperative [please note all you fabulous citizens who perennially insist that recreational use of marijuana is harmless].

On another occasion as I was walking down the hallway, a female student whom I did not know came up and yelled something directly into my ear with all her might. Although I filed a report, the reader will get an additional sense of the tone of the school.

The deans at the school told me about slashings during the warmer weather by students during the passing of classes. Students would be slashed with Gillette razor blades, and then the blades were tossed out the hallway windows that were opened six inches once the weather became warmer. Or there would sometimes be stabbings by students who were able to get sharpened toothbrushes past the metal detectors. But the sharpened plastic of the toothbrush handles could stab almost as well as a metal knife.

The published behavior code of the Department of Education was consistently not enforced. In fact, the misbehavior described in the book was actually a description of the norm for the school because cooperative, good behavior was the exception.

Infractions that would normally be punished (the New York City Code of Discipline does not use the word "punish" one time, but instead lists "consequences") are so pervasive that one can truly say that anarchy reigned. One teacher, Mr. Zen, an English teacher who boasted of his daily Buddhist meditations, gave all students grades of 90 or above. If they came and did not work, he would give them 95 or higher; but if they only came to class once, they would get a consolation prize of 90-92. In this way, he felt he was mocking a destructive system. But, is it really necessary at this point to draw your attention to the fact that Mr. Zen was never called to task for this ridiculous behavior? He was never reprimanded and never told to change his ways. The message to all of us was, in fact, to emulate his behavior lacking in all integrity. In Hellhole High and increasingly across New York City (and in many school districts across our country), if you fail the course, you do not fail. If you misbehave, you are not punished, or not punished severely enough. If you do not pass a state test, your score is manipulated upwards. In six years at HH, there was never any NY State reversals of the New York State

Regents scores although there was massive moving of scores from 55 to 65. Further, funding for the schools is based on attendance, and this teacher was informed by a colleague in the attendance office that the attendance was falsified every day at the direction of the principal.

OVERSEERS OF EDUCATION MUST LEARN TO SEE

It is ironic that Hellhole High where I worked was roundly criticized by newspapers, TV, and even the State Department of Education, yet no really profound changes for the better were made during the six year period I was there. In fact, for a two year period, the school was intensely observed by state observers because of the school's presence on New York State's SURR List (Schools Under Registration Review). Yet, the many observers sent to the schools never reported on the basic issues that I and many of my co-teachers considered to be important. Instead, they focused mostly on curricular changes, making some good changes, but also many changes that were politically correct or educationally trendy yet without significance. One of my co-teachers referred to the changes that were recommended as "cosmetic." As further proof of this comment, Hellhole High was determined to be a failing school and closed. Three small academy schools were opened on the same site to replace the failed school. However, in a few short years, the three replacement schools were deemed "failing schools" and replaced by four new small schools. Is this anything less than patent corruption?

It seemed clear to me that these observers and consultants believed that if instructional strategies were sufficiently revised all other problems would automatically be resolved or at least significantly ameliorated. The belief that curricular reform is the key to educational reform is far from true, and I felt that the consultants who came to our school had little understanding of the day-to-day reality in which we worked. It was clear to us that those who came to evaluate the school could not survive even one week in the school. We had seen too many talented, fine teachers flee our halls to have any illusions about what we were facing every day. The Holy Scriptures tell us "the truth will set you free." If this is true, then surely it is ungodly to spin a web of lies and half-truths in the name of educational progress and reform.

FOUL IMPRESSIONS

If you went into the inner city high school where I spent six years of my work life, you would find a pit of chaos and ignorance that would make your head spin.

The students would be congregating ("chillin'") in the hallways 10-15 minutes into every class period. The boys would be making lewd remarks and gestures to the girls, and the girls would be doing the same thing. Sometimes the boys literally would drag the girls down the hallway floor while the girls shrieked and cursed delightedly. One day I watched as a girl walked backwards down the hallway holding her crotch and shrieking, "You wouldn't know how to use your ---- in my ----, you#@#!!" The boy was yelling back some obscenities mixed with a street jive language that was unintelligible to me.

SCHOOL CONSTRUCTION: HOUSES OF THEFT

What about school construction? Sounds good, right? Noble, right? Is it not beautiful to contemplate more houses of learning? Or, renovated and modernized school buildings? Well that's what I thought before I saw the work of the School Construction Authority in New York City. After eight-plus years of renovating our school with a cost estimate ballooning from $29 million to $70-$90 million (one school mind you), they still were so far behind on the job that temporary, mobile classrooms had to be put in the school courtyard to accommodate the students. When asked by this writer about the delays, costs, mess, shoddy workmanship, etc., the project manager replied, "We're right on schedule."

After more than six years work, the roof still leaked (one of the custodians told me that the gutters for the roofs were permanently clogged and were not included in the renovation contract). A piece of the ceiling in one of my classes in a newly renovated wing came crashing to the floor barely missing a student. The wild students broke the handles and locks of most of the new doors, but there was no provision in the construction contracts for the repair or replacement of the handles (it was explained to me that they had to be included in a contract because they were not a type of hardware that you could just go out and buy in a hardware store). The cheap floors were filthy and scuffed and uncleanable less than a year after they were laid.

"WE'RE GETTING BETTER"

In one inner city high school where I taught, the results of the state examinations in Social Studies were an abysmal "high" of about 20% passing the state Regents (more difficult) and another 20% passing the RCT (easier). Even these paltry results were the effects of either direct falsification of scores or grading so easy as to be, for all practical purposes, falsification. What lies! What hypocrisy! The exams are forwarded to the state for review. In the entire six years, I never once heard of one case of the NY State Regents reversing the results of any of our tests. We were not audited once. Is this not an example of complicity in a lie? THE SYSTEM IS PROGRAMMED TO "GO

ALONG." It's surely a case of the king has no clothes. Everyone is either outright lying or going along as part of job survival or out of the self-serving belief that by going along, passing the unqualified, they are actually "helping kids."

This teacher had the unpleasant duty of telling the principal that the assistant principal in social studies was simply erasing Regents scores and replacing them with higher scores than those assigned by the teachers who had read them. The assistant principal later complained to me that I should have come to her and discussed the matter first. Wouldn't that be a little like going to Bonnie and Clyde and saying, "Gee guys, you know, I noticed you've been robbing banks, and that is not right you know...."

The principal in his usual sidestepping, evasive, non-think way (he was a thinker, he knew better) said that if one of the two readers' scores was changed by a third reader then the third reader should add his or her score and initialize the score like the other readers. This answer was itself unethical and wrong, since the rules called for two readers and not three, and third readers could not overrule either or both of the other two readers. Thus his "ethical answer" really did not address the issue, and allowed the changing to go on as long as the changer included his or her initials.

I was not ready to go over the principal's head with this, and so the practice continued with a phony ethical disguise. Then the next term, the principal was out, three new principals were in, and everyone went right back to the same old phony erasure system with grading that made a mockery of the whole process and was, in my opinion, 100% illegal.

WHO CARES ABOUT THE GOOD STUDENTS?

Despite all the rhetoric about improving the poor school where I taught, there was little concern for that element of the student population that demonstrated academic ability and a true desire to learn. Despite all the talk about the viability of the African-American student and his right to compete in the marketplace of education and ideas, the successful students in the school did not receive the attention I felt they deserved.

When this author suggested to the principal at one of the high schools within our campus that the parents of the ten or twenty best students be invited to a meeting to help them help their children improve their prospects for getting into a better college, I was rebuffed. Why? The principal told me that many of the students were illegals anyway and probably would not have the papers to go to a "good college" (understand by this -- a college outside New York City community colleges where they can register even if they are illegal).

Also, a faculty committee recommended to the principal that a position of college advisor be created, but she insisted it was work already being covered adequately on a part-time basis. Meanwhile the top student in the graduating class told me he probably would not be going on to college because his parents were moving back to Jamaica. No one but me seemed to care that this student in the midst of a terrible environment had received five grades of 99 or 100 on his report card; yet probably would not go to college. In fact, he and two other top students were disqualified from being valedictorians because they were in the school for only two years rather than four. I believed that the real reason was that two of those three were from an Indian rather than an African heritage.

My question: was this a school the authorities were trying to reform, to upgrade, or was this a school which they were using to perpetuate their own selfish ends?

GRADUATION: MORE POSSIBILITY THAN PROBABILITY

With the cozy relationship among the administrators, other forms of incompetence were tolerated, and even applauded. Imagine that five weeks into the term, the coordinator of administration boasted to the faculty that programs for the term were finalized. Students were finally assigned to programs and rosters which would remain in place for the term. These rosters should be finalized by the third day of school or the end of the first week at the very latest.

During the entire time of adjusting the rosters-- fully one-quarter of the term--students were reassigned from class to class--one day appearing and another day disappearing from one's class. One teacher mildly asked if the teachers could help in any way to bring about an earlier finalization of scheduling. This question was met with a defensive barrage of excuses about why the four or five weeks was necessary and "couldn't be helped" and was even "quite good considering circumstances." What about progress through school? In the inner city school where I taught, out of 650 students on roll, the school graduated only 50. Many of those students had been there five or more years. Besides, rumor had it that actually there were only to have been 35-40 graduates, but that by speedy and unauthorized changing of grades, the higher number of 45-50 "made it" to graduation.

At the end of my third year at the school, I knew for a fact that one of my students in economics only showed up for about three or four classes all term, and failed my course. Yet, on graduation day, he received his diploma. This happened despite the fact that one cannot graduate from a high school New York City without passing the senior course in economics, and no grade can be changed without notifying the teacher in writing. Yet, I was never notified. Most teachers believed that these changes took place frequently, but wisdom--survival--indicated that one not challenge or try to follow up on these matters.

During my last two years at the school, only two students managed to graduate with the higher Regents Diploma. These students were exceptional in that the school, while a New York State high school, did not offer sufficient language courses for students to qualify for a Regents diploma even if they succeeded in passing the Regents exams in their other subjects. The assistant principal shrugged this off by noting that since the students do not pass enough of the other subjects the issue of offering Spanish was moot. "They wouldn't get the Regents diploma anyhow!"

Even with the phony graduations, the overall number of graduates was still dismal. Remember, students are taking courses at night and in the summers to make up failures and they still are not graduating. Is this not the greatest all-American waste of tax money on the face of the earth? Imagine this--students are going through high school piecemeal and still do not make it. Take student A. She takes 15 courses her freshman year and fails five. Of those five, she takes two in summer school and passes one. That means she is four courses behind. Then let us say in the Fall term of the following school year, she makes up two and takes five other new courses, while at the same time taking another of her four failures as a repeat at night. This means she still would have one outstanding failure. Then, suppose the student passes two of the three she is making up, but fails two of the five "new" courses. By the end of the Fall term of her second year, the student would still be behind the eight ball to the tune of four failures.

In addition, with all the record-keeping complexity this causes, the student would likely be programmed in the Spring either into a course she has already passed, or into a course for which she is not eligible (having failed an earlier course in the sequence), or not into a course she needs to make up. Failure becomes an administrative morass which creates an atmosphere of total confusion.

With students advancing through their education in this helter-skelter way, this writer concludes that a voucher system and privatization is inevitable. What I have described is gross mismanagement and, in my opinion, is so far gone as deserving to be called corruption. Students who will never graduate are being catered to and given so much so-called individualized treatment as to run the costs and the entire orderliness of the process into the ground. I have written "so-called individualized treatment" because it is based on a dishonest communication. It is implied to the student that if you make up this and that you will go through high school piecemeal and eventually graduate, when in fact as I already noted, very few get to wear the cap and gown.

A rejoinder might be: do you want all these students to drop out? My answer is that the students would be more fairly treated if they understood that they had to pass the course when they took it rather than believing that their "hope" lies in repeating the course at night, during summer schools, or another term in the daytime. These "options" act as disincentives to make an all-out effort; and I suggest they contribute to the "let down" mentality which causes students to cut, be late, not do homework, not study, and direct their attention away from the educational process. Further, there should be earlier job opportunities for students who simply have no academic motivation or gifts, but who might benefit from resuming their educations in a few years when they are more settled and mature.

WHAT ABOUT LATENESS AND CUTTING AT SCHOOL?

When a teacher at a faculty meeting suggested that the school was lax on cutting, the principal suggested that anyone who thought that "must have blinders on." She had been telling the teachers that they should handle cutting as an individual matter-- calling parents, or keeping late books and penalizing the students. She told us that it was not a school-wide issue. Further, over a period of five-plus years, the teachers were told by a host of different super-visors (the school was constantly being reorganized) that students cut classes because our lessons were boring, and if we did a better job they would not cut.

This claim was patently untrue. Students in first period routinely cut. Many students told this teacher, even in front of their mothers, that it was just "too early" for them to get up or get out. I asked one young man (17-1/2 years old) if he owned an alarm clock. His mother interjected, "He certainly does, but before it rings, he pulls the plug!"

One of the more effective teachers received a computer printout of cuts during the term and found that more than 75% had cut three or more times, with 50% having as many as ten cuts. Cutting was not the exception, but the rule!

Teachers were advised to take measures against cutting, including calls home to parents, a late book to be signed by the entering (late) students, and penalties for lateness. Despite admonitions to the students, and penalties, the hallways were filled with milling students 10-15 minutes after each period began. When asked to move off toward class by security, teachers, and/or deans, the students would ignore the encouragement, and pretend they did not hear a word--just continue their joking and talking as though the school official and the requirement to go to class was non-existent. If the suggestion to move on should become more forceful, perhaps to the point of interrupting the students' conversations, the students might say "o.k.," but then continue not to go to class. After all this goading and prodding, the hallway crowds would finally break up and students would arrive late for their classes.

Yes. It's against the city code of discipline to cut classes; yet in the inner city school and outside the inner city, it was part of the student culture, and cutting was totally accepted. To the best of my knowledge, no student in six years was disciplined by the school administration for cutting. The question they asked was: how can you suspend or expel a student for cutting when you want him or her to be in school? How can you punish a student for being chronically late when this punishment causes the student to cut, and/or eventually drop out? Thus, some schools are now using in-house suspension. But these questions miss the whole point: the goal of education is to teach students the subject and to build character. The problem with cutting and lateness is not that they are not in the building or not in the classroom (being physically present in a facility is in itself meaningless!), but that they are 1) disrupting the functioning of the school and society, 2) failing to obey the authorities, 3) not placing a sufficiently high value on education, and 4) not doing the right thing.

What about lateness? Can you imagine a line of 20-30 students waiting to be admitted at 11:00 a.m.? When this subject was brought up at a faculty meeting, teachers were told it was "illegal" to deny the late students admission. Is this true? This author never checked. Yet, we teachers believed that this admission was an excuse to inflate the school's daily attendance figure, which was the basis for funding of the school's budget.

If it is truly illegal to turn these students away, should this "law" not be taken off the books so our schools may be properly administered? Why was the school's administration not advocating for this change?

Why is the message sent out to teachers that the teachers are to be blamed for the failing schools? At the same time, the students, not the teachers, are given the lion's share of credit for their success at the few top-notch high schools. We teachers are doing the best we can under difficult circumstances. Why have the schools been allowed to degenerate to this level? Teachers are more captives of the system, while the administrators of the schools, pandering to the public, continue to claim with feigned ingenuousness that they are doing their best.

Of course many teachers are bored and listless, but it seems to me that this is more of an effect than a cause of the demoralization within the schools. The teachers' union makes a pretense of caring, but ultimately it is in collusion with the status quo mentality and the explosion of uncaring management that marks the schools. Since October 31, 2009 until the writing of this book (2014), the teachers of New York City were without a contract with the New York City government; yet not one word about this appeared at any time in any union communications with the membership. What could represent a greater and more glaring failure of the union than this? Under the strange and perverse Mayor Doomsday and a sycophantic union, changes in the workplace rules governing the schools were typically changed by *ad hoc* agreements between the teachers' union and the Mayor. When workplace rules are in a contract, the members have a chance to vote upon the contract. But when they are agreed upon behind closed doors in a collusion between the union and the Mayor, then the members have no say and the democratic aspect of their service is undermined.

LAVATORIES: UNTOUCHED BY HUMAN HANDS

The lavatories were few and far between. Sometimes one would have to walk one to one and one-half city blocks of corridors to relieve oneself. The stench and filth of the lavatories and lack of regular supplies of soap, toilet paper, and towels would make any civilized person cringe.

The lavatory in the front office would typically have four or five people waiting in line to use it, and in keeping with the latest unisex trends, most of the bathrooms were used by both male and female teachers. The principal at one school was heard joking about how offensive visitors to the school found the odors in the Men Teachers' bathroom on the first floor.

Sometimes the doors of the teacher lavatories were left unlocked or were unlocked by teachers for use by both male and female students.

In a better school where I taught, the amenities were somewhat better, but the boys bathrooms had no doors, and the passersby, including thousands of girls, would have to see the boys lined up behind a wooden partition urinating.

Once my department chairman personally put out a fire in the girls' bathroom. The girls had put lighter fluid on a wooden seat, and set fire to the seat. Then they managed to seal shut the door of the stall. My chairman had to stand on an adjacent toilet seat and squirt the fire extinguisher onto the blazing seat.

Other times one would enter bathrooms to find the windows open and unclosable giving a view of the bathroom interior to other windows in the school complex. Or sometimes the window would be wide open in the middle of winter with the cold air blasting in (at least there was temporary relief from the zoo-like odor).

At one point during construction on the campus, so many toilets were within blocked-off construction areas that portable johns were brought in and put outside in the school courtyard for use of students and teachers. Even in winter these unheated facilities were to be used. Further, the company renting the johns did not clean them. Only when one teacher called the toilet company was a truck dispatched to clean out the putrid wastes that were collecting in excess. Yet, these "temporary" amenities remained filthy and, I am convinced, were a health hazard if not an outright cause of disease among those using them.

After six years, do you think the situation improved? Hardly. The bathroom in the teachers' lounge had no catch on the door, nor did the one booth of the single toilet facility for teachers. The facility was used by both male and female teachers, and one had to knock to enter. Many times the teachers forgot to knock or their knock was not heard much to the embarrassment of the person using the room as well as the one entering. The room was filthy, and the unclosable window was the only relief.

NO ASSEMBLIES: RACIAL UNITY BUT NOT SCHOOL UNITY

In ten years of teaching in New York, there were some special assembly programs, but no regular assemblies. In no high school where I taught was the school alma mater taught and sung. In no high school where I taught was the Star Spangled Banner sung except at graduation. This was true in schools where there was a diversity of ethnic backgrounds, and schools where there was not.

At no time in that high school or any other high school where I taught was any American national holiday celebrated--e.g. Presidents' Day, Thanksgiving, Memorial Day, Columbus Day, or Mother's Day. Columbus Day is commonly scorned by students and faculty not of Italian descent as Columbus has been vilified by historical revisionists for the past two decades. The other national holidays are simply ignored as though they did not exist. This is true even in social studies departments, even though Black History Month or Women's History Month are sometimes (not always) given special attention.

Only after one teacher complained was the Star Spangled Banner included in award assemblies. Although these high schools are public, i.e., supported by taxpayers of all ethnicities, all national respect and loyalty was thrown out the window.

(By the way, in the District Plan for School Based Planning, the model for school governance in place in many high schools, it is stated that students are being prepared for "global citizenship." It would seem that preparation for U.S. citizenship is being by-passed or is considered so "obvious" as to not bear mention. [It's not!])

Again, what is wrong with celebrating America's feast of the harvest, Thanksgiving? You know, every immigrant child, whether from the former Soviet Union or from the Caribbean or from Asia has been brought to America for a new life. Most will remain here and not go back to their lands of origin. Does it really help them to exclude the national observances from their education as a proper part of their education? We all have our roots, and it is right and fit to love and honor our roots, but when, at the same time, we reject the honored traditions and observances of our adopted country, we have done both ourselves and our country a disservice.

VIOLENCE: TIANANMEN SQUARE IN REVERSE

Despite the fact that one of the schools where I taught had eighteen unarmed peace officers and two city police officers assigned full-time, violence still proliferated. During the first two years I was there, there were no metal detectors at the entrance, and a spirit of meanness and violence were almost tangible.

Yet, even four years after the metal detectors were installed, a female student was shot in the foot by an assailant right outside the school. On another occasion, there was a riot involving over 300 students about one block from the school after the school day ended. Police trying to break up the riot were attacked by students who felt they were unfairly pushed by police as they tried to break through the crowds to the point where the fighting was heaviest. Then these poor children who were only standing up for their "rights" were arrested. My oh my, what an insensitive and brutal police force!

During my first year at the school there was a full-scale riot on campus between the Jamaican and the Haitian students. Rocks and heavy tools from

135

the on-campus construction site were thrown. Windows were smashed. Trash cans were set on fire. Riot police were called in, and the school was closed 1-1/4 hours early.

Believe it or not, not one word about this event was stated over the public address system, nor were there any assemblies to discuss the mayhem with the student body. Nor did the riot appear on the evening news or in the New York papers. Nor, I might add, were there any punishments. Six students were arrested and booked by the police. Yet, at our faculty meeting, the principal earnestly told us that after hours of pleading and talking with the police he was able to gain the release of the students and have their arrests expunged. This pitiful, gutless, ostrich-like principal it seemed actually believed that this extraordinary leniency actually helped the situation!

Mr. Deceit would be seen by me walking down the halls berated and cursed at by a student, and all he would say was to ask the student to walk a little faster as he was late for an appointment. Certainly, it is good for a principal in New York to have a thick skin as far as some of the foul-mouths and criminals are concerned, but this personal virtue does not make good policy. The principal should not take the cursing personally, but for the good of the student and for the sake of school order such behavior by students should not be tolerated--at all--ever!

I saw this same principal while attempting to break up a fight thrown on the floor by a student. And on another occasion when a girl in one of my classes refused to show him her identification card, he had her removed from the class only to be returned the next day. As a new teacher, I was so ashamed about what had happened in my class that I went home and prayed for three hours, and later apologized to the principal for "my" [sic] student." How innocent and naïve I was. He just shrugged and said, "it's nothing." Ho-hum. All in a day's work.

By the end of my first year of teaching, it became unequivocally clear to me that this kind of student behavior, even up to and including wanton rioting, was completely tolerated. If the Tiananmen Square massacre was an outrage at the repressive end of the spectrum, then surely my school's response to bad behavior was equally outrageous, though at the complete opposite end of the spectrum.

How much further can the liberal, ultra-permissive philosophy of education go?

CAN SCHOOL SPIRIT BE BOUGHT?

Lastly, what is "school spirit?" It is an intangible, and it cannot successfully be reduced to statistics anymore than teacher morale. A statistical model can be set up, but it will be flawed. For example, two Christmas' ago my family and I went to the Christmas musical production at the high school where I was teaching. I was surprised to note that outside the music department, I was the only faculty member present. To me, that is an interesting statistic -- one out of 250+ teachers. At the risk of oversimplifying, I inferred that there was a tremendous lack of school spirit in the faculty, and that my everyday observation that the faculty was demoralized was correct. Now, if we were to set up a program whereby every teacher who attended would receive $200, then surely more would attend. Assuming that 100 then attended, the program would cost $20,000. Would we then have demonstrated "school spirit"?

THE HELLISH MIDDLE YEARS

In ten years of teaching, I never met one high school teacher who had taught in middle school or junior high school who was not thankful every day of his or her life to be out of that middle school hell. I substituted in a number of middle and junior high schools, and know others who teach there.

It comes as no surprise to learn that the gap in reading and math scores between the public and private schools in New York widens during the junior high school years. Also, there is a tremendous drop in the percentage passing when the 8th grade scores are compared with the 4th grade scores. The junior highs are bedlam and hellish. There are very few that have any educational merit. In one school where I substituted, the class was going wild. The principal entered the room, and told me that I was not in control of the class. I agreed, and said, "Since you are the principal, I'm sure they will come to order if you direct them." The principal turned away from me and walked out of the room.

At the same school, in one class I collected two armloads of assorted chains and pipes (these were from 6th graders). I brought this load down to the principal at the end of the school day, and told him that I had confiscated them from students. He asked me for the names of the students, and I told him that they would not give me their names, and that I could not take attendance. "Well, without the names," he said, "it is impossible for me to do anything." This was patently false since the entire class could have been and should have been punished.

The junior high and middle schools in New York are preparatory schools for high school disorder. When they enter in 9th grade in most schools most of the ninth graders are deviant, chaotic, hyper, have no concentration span (about 20 seconds), and ACCOMPLISH NOTHING. Except for the very best high schools, teachers long to accumulate enough seniority so they do not get ninth grade teaching assignments.

EVEN OSTRICHES KNOW WHEN TO RUN

After teaching for only ten years in diverse educational settings -- that is, teaching students who are "at risk" and teaching others who are among New York's most gifted, I noticed something: the destructive problems afflicting today's youth are almost totally ignored. There are programs in some schools, but the problems students have are not addressed on a school-wide basis.

What are some of the danger areas for today's youth?

Abortion

Addiction to Internet pornography.

Alcohol abuse.

Bullying by peers and other forms of criminal violence within the school or in the community.

Cigarette smoking.

Conflicts within the family.

Drug use and abuse.

Fear of the future.

Inability to concentrate.

Lack of a family.

Lack of sleep.

Loneliness and insecurity.

Moral perversions.

Sexual activity outside of marriage, promiscuity, and sexually transmitted diseases.

Suicide.

In ten years of teaching, I did not encounter one school-wide attempt to counteract any of the above issues. There were no assemblies -- no, not one -- on any of the above topics. There were no posters or school-wide propaganda campaigns against any of the above.

Sexually transmitted diseases were addressed in health education, though not mainly from the point of abstinence, nor from the view that love and marriage is the greatest defense against STDs. These courses never stressed that the family – marriage between a man and a woman -- is the basic building block of civilization.

I looked through one of the health education booklets used in one of the courses, and [can you believe it?] there was a page telling the students that the size of penises is unrelated to sexual satisfaction. Yes, I'm sure this is a comfort to thousands of morons who are asking themselves that question. In the same book, marriage and family is treated as an "option" (that is, the students are told that some people choose to wait until they are married to have sex and that this choice is o.k.). Marriage and family life is one of many choices, a choice to be tolerated, but certainly not to be idealized or desired by all. Get it. Someone who makes that choice is to be tolerated [sic], not disparaged and run out of town. Yikes! This is a formula for destruction.

WHAT TYPE OF SCHOOLS DO WE WANT?

Do we want schools where there is passionate making out in the stairwells and in the hallways? Do we want schools where suggestive non-events like "Pajama Day" are sending the wrong signals to the student body? Do we want schools where shows are performed like "Hair," that was originally famous for full frontal nudity, obscenities, and racial slurs? Do we really want health education classes were the students are given instructions on how to put a condom on a cucumber or a banana? One health education textbook lying in one classroom asked the profound question: Is it true that women really get more sexual satisfaction from a bigger penis? This was not in Playboy magazine mind you, but in a textbook! In one high school where this author taught, there was a Mr. and Ms. High School contest. Photos of male students who were com- peting were posted in the corridor outside the student cafeteria where the boys were wearing jock straps and flexing their muscles. The girls at the contest were also wearing the skimpiest of bikinis.

On one occasion, I was sitting marking papers after school, and one of the teachers was inter-viewing/coaching one of his students about a research paper he was doing. I could not believe my ears, and asked the boy, who was sitting just to my right, how old he was. "Seventeen," he said. I then turned to my colleague, and said "Mr. Queerface, I will have to report this to the Assistant Principal." You see, he and the boy were planning a research where the student would go to a whorehouse to ask a series of research questions to the Russian and Asian whores in the brothel. (Amazingly, the parents took the side of the research once the principal became involved, but the project was stopped because there was fear that the place might be raided by the police, and if the student were there, it would put the school in a bad light. Great reason, right?!)

The dignity of learning is adversely affected by these activities, and among the majority of students, who are not drawn to these modes of self-expression, their presence on campus may produce a range of negative responses from embarrassment to profound disturbance. Believe it or not, many teens are not yet comfortable with their sexuality, and the above-mentioned vulgar and ungodly activities are doing nothing to dispel their fears and confusions.

Another moral issue facing the New York public high schools is the absence of singing of the "Star Spangled Banner" or the recitation of the Pledge of Allegiance to the flag except at graduation. Other patriotic songs like "My Country Tis of Thee," "America the Beautiful," or "God Bless America" were never sung once in over 20 years that I spent in the schools. These time-honored expressions of national identity transcend all political ideologies whether they be "liberal" or "conservative." How can it not be right to honor and respect the country where most of the students expect to spend their lives until the day of death? The U.S.A. is where they will work, raise their families, and live out their destiny, and where they will establish the social, intellectual, economic, political, and spiritual ideas to be passed on to future generations of AMERICANS. Further, the recitation and singing of these patriotic expressions is moral because we do not as yet live in a "new world order" [advocated by ex-President George Bush] or a "global village" which inspires Mrs. Clinton. Whether or not we believe the nation-state concept has outlived its usefulness, we are living in a world where the nation-state concept is the working concept and still valid.

Lastly, there needs to be a review of all the human sexuality programs whether they are sex education courses or programs for the distribution of birth control or STD devices or abortion counseling (if it exists on campus). Is sexuality being treated as mere self-gratification within a context of "safety," or are the values of modesty, self-control, and abstinence outside of marriage given the priority they deserve? Are we encouraging commitment and fulfillment, or are we encouraging gross licentiousness? Are we encouraging love and marriage, or are we encouraging the moral decay and loneliness that uncommitted eroticism brings? Are we encouraging monogamy, or are we encouraging male and female Don Juanism?

PART THREE: THE IDEOLOGICAL LEFT IS ON THE MARCH, ESPECIALLY IN SOCIAL STUDIES EDUCATION. NO KIDDING.

REVISING TRUTH CREATES CULTURAL QUICKSAND

The glorification of the victims of history has gone beyond the point of seeking compassion for them and trying to assure that what happened to them will never happen again. The cult of victims – mainly women, minorities, and the poor – has become lodged in a matrix of philosophical relativism bordering on anarchism, combined with a radical redefinition of all that has been positive in history. According to this new "deconstructivist" vision, successful human activity through the ages, and especially in Europe and America during the past five hundred years, is guided by an underlying principle of oppression and cruel exploitation. We find a kind of updated Marxism where "class struggle" has been redefined as a gender and racial struggle with serious economic implications.

Capitalism is not so much failed because of its economic hegemony, as under traditional Marxism, but because it is inherently supportive of extreme sexual and racial bias. Thus, the exploitation of the have nots by the haves is far more sinister and deeply embedded in the wrongs of society than the original Marxists ever imagined. Communism has failed – not because communism was basically wrongheaded -- but because the underlying concepts on which it was based did not go far enough in detailing the implications of capitalism in its sexist and racist dimensions. The fact that the capitalistic system was from the beginning in the hands of white male racist, sexist, and homophobic individuals was not understood by the original Marxists, and that's why they ultimately failed to change the world.

The new radicals, the New New Left [hereafter referred to as NNL] (the "new left" was that left which followed the New Deal lefties, and was characteristic of the 1950's and 1960's lefties – like Students for a Democratic Society) imagines that the communist egalitarian ideal can be achieved now in a new way, a way Marx, Engels, Lenin, and Stalin never envisaged. There will be a complete revision of the working definitions of society, of the legal structure, and of the relations between schools, the workplace, and government. The idea of a mixed economy will be widened to violate the corporate concept.

The goal of the NNL is to transform our society into a communist society without a violent revolution, without overthrowing the capitalistic class, without a dictatorship of the proletariat, and without using the language of communism, even without using the word "communism" itself. Gradually the enlightenment ideas of natural rights and inalienable rights to life, liberty, and the pursuit of happiness will be eroded. How? By shifting from a concept of individual rights (which are the basis of the democratic revolutions that have formed our world) to collective rights. We shall see a continuing attempt to form a quasi-fascist coordination of government and private enterprise, with a certain leveling tendency caused by a softening of fascist nationalism under the new rubric of "globalization."

You and I will count for less and the state and global priorities will count for more. There will be greater and greater emphasis on "equality" and less and less emphasis on "liberty" or "life" or the "pursuit of happiness." Thus, the NNL hopes to move to a new communism (without "communism"), a new totalitarianism, and a permanent attack upon the individual as a sacred entity.

You see, "collective rights" is a concept whereby your rights and mine derive from membership in a group. Jane Doe's rights will come primarily from the fact that she is in a group – women. Someone else's rights will be based increasingly in his or her ethnic grouping, i.e., Asian, African-American, Hispanic, etc. Thus, the Constitution provides for states' rights and individual rights, but there will be new, competing units of rights-deserving groups. Also, implied in this is that certain groups will lose rights – groups such as white males or people of European descent.

The NNL believes that the underlying concepts that formed this country had no absolute basis in truth, but were emanations of a vulgar power play by the founding fathers, an elite group whose only desire, either conscious or unconscious, was to establish a racist, sexist society where the money and power remained eternally in the hands of English speaking, white male Protestants. The fact that the founding fathers risked their "lives, fortunes, and sacred honor" in support of their philosophical and political goals is dismissed as so much rhetoric.

The fact that the founding fathers started and built a new country that has proved to be viable for more than two centuries seems to carry little weight with the NNL. The fact that mechanisms have existed to correct abuses in the system seems not to touch their view that the system itself is fundamentally flawed. The fact that the United States of America has done more to promote freedom, security, and hope in the world than any other country is rebuffed as unacceptable self-congratulation. The fact that people from every continent flock here to take advantage of the many opportunities afforded to all people strikes the NNL elitists as an aberration. These stupid immigrants, according to the NNL, don't know any better than to believe in the American ideal. We'll teach them the facts. First they'll vote Democratic; then we shall radicalize them as part of the new mass movement against freedom.

The educated elite of this country still want to be the intellectual "vanguard of the proletariat" described in Marxist theory. They want to conquer the minds of the people through the education system, including higher education, then move into government (they already have), and finally reign supreme against those monstrous profiteers in the business world. The NNL realizes that beginning with violent revolution is the wrong starting point for the revolution they desire. Rather, in the United States, the starting point is in the minds of the people.

The idea of rights that are absolute, that cut across all classifications of people, will be and are being attacked by a new relativism. The new relativism is more far-reaching than earlier relativisms in that it even debunks the possibility of objectivity in science. In fact, there is no objectivity in the new relativism, sometimes called "post-modernism," but it does not disintegrate into nihilism because it adheres to the idea of power as an underlying force that keeps everything from, so to speak, flying apart.

The idea of "empowerment" in the new liberal-leftist dictionary goes far beyond the classical American ideal of equality of opportunity, but unashamedly mobilizes communities to use government for personal gain – government not only gives you opportunities, but it guarantees you success. It invests in you because you have political clout. Then it advises you, or, basically, makes sure that you do everything you should do to avoid failure, and then it gives you tax breaks, and finally, if all else fails, it gives you government contracts to assure your success.

Meanwhile, hiring priorities are set so that certain groups are given preference, and the gravy train goes on….with full governmental approval and sanctions and support.

When studying political science in college, I was taught by a professor who was a student of the great democratic thinker Prof. Robert Strauz-Hupé. In the course he emphasized that while fascism and communism were so opposed to each other, in practice they both seemed to arrive at the same point. He asked us to imagine that they both began at the top of a circle, moving in opposite directions; yet, by the time they had completed their movement, at the bottommost point of the circle they were at the same place.

How do the schools fit into the big picture of the above-described changes?

Victimized Groups Define America: The schools have selected certain victimized groups as demonstrating the failure of America, and it is almost impossible to present an alternative view to the students. The point is: America is not a failure, and the groups identified as failures [sic] are largely failures because of their own poor choices.

Independent Thought Is Discouraged: In my classes, I polled the students in the Gore v. Bush election, and fully 99% of the students said they would have voted for Gore. If 60% had said this, I would not have been alarmed. That alone would have meant a landslide victory for Gore. Well, o.k., it's a free country. But when almost 100% identify with only one of the two candidates, then I think we have a demonstration of how far the NNL has made inroads into the minds and hearts of the people and of the youth in particular.

Education Is Replaced With Skills Training: The emphasis on skills and skill sets as opposed to a body of knowledge (sometimes referred to as 'cultural literacy'), creativity, critical thinking requiring analysis, synthesis, and logic, is bringing down students to an unprecedented level of ignorance. Job readiness is the key to education as there is more and more pigeonholing of students, and students are more dependent and less ready for the work world than ever. In Hellhole High School, students were sometimes assigned half a day to a "Resource Room" [sic] where they would spend most of their time "learning" how to fill out job application forms or just hanging out with their friends. Education is totally geared to channeling people into corporate jobs and make-work government jobs. The importance of all in education that does not immediately bear on making a living (such as history, literature, math, languages, etc.) is minimized by the corporate/government partnership. Further, the student who is less able is led by the nose into the work world.

Students lose all opportunity to develop as educated independent people. They are introduced to some little function they can perform in a business and are monumentally supported in doing that function. If they are ever taken out of that support system, they will not be able to function, and will be worse off than they would have been had they never been introduced to those jobs. The better students still have to fend for themselves within a competitive context while the poorer students have their lives increasingly managed for them by government and business. The masses of the poor ethnics are always shouting "Freedom Now!" but the very programs they support are, ironically and sadly, stealing what freedoms they have.

Instead of promoting and supporting true freedom, the system is capitalizing on their helplessness and the NNL program of redefinition whereby the unskilled are given the opportunity to advance and skip the skills that everybody else presumably needs.

Teachers Are Consciously Promoting Leftist Ideology: One member of the NNL came up to me with a mocking smile on his face. He said, "Communism may have collapsed in the Soviet Union, but it is alive and well in this high school." The reader should not be surprised that this writer is still seeing red [a perfect idiom, isn't it].

Despite the fact that teachers are required to select textbooks from an approved list available to the schools and within the departments, I know that some social studies teachers dispense with the text-books and rely predominantly on a text by Howard Zinn, A Peoples History of the United States. The title alone should tell the reader what the bias of the book is. Prof. Zinn was a self-proclaimed com-munist in the Boston area in the 1960's and 1970's.

Indifference Is The Weapon of Choice Against The National Entity Known As The United States of America: In ten years of teaching in the public high schools of New York City, I do not recall the celebration of one official national holiday on a school-wide basis, including Dr. Martin Luther King's birthday. Can you imagine? Presidents' Day is ignored. Mother's Day and Father's Day are ignored. Christmas and Easter vacations have been replaced with Winter Break and Spring Break. Thanksgiving once in awhile gets a passing comment on the public address system.

Part of the reason is that assemblies often present a tremendous security problem to the schools. The students can become rowdy or even riotous. However, beyond that practical issue lies the agenda of the NNL to discredit the government and institutions of the United States. They do not always openly criticize the U.S. and its institutions, but simply by ignoring those institutional factors which identify the youth with the nation they instill a fundamental disrespect for the country.

THE OLD LIBERALS SPAWNED THE NEW NEW LEFT

In Roger Rosenblatt's interesting slice of anecdotal history, *Coming Apart: A Memoir of the Harvard Wars of 1969,* he expresses a belief that the radicals who took over Harvard's buildings in the 1960's had the long-term effect of driving out the "good liberals" from the halls of academe, and that those radicals irrevocably smeared the otherwise good label of liberalism.

The so-called good liberals of Harvard spawned the radicalism that followed. In 1969 the Harvard faculty harbored gays and straights who found nothing unethical about seducing and cohabiting with students. Heavy drinking, nervous breakdowns, and divorce were common. Smoking marijuana in many circles was considered sophisticated. It seems that the so-called good liberals loved the aesthetics and freedom of Western civilization, but the inherited moral values were spurned. So the radicals took over, and the old liberals are gradually being pushed out by the New New Left. Why feel sorry for them? As you sow so shall you reap.

LEFTIST TEXTBOOKS AND WORLD WAR I[13]

As a high school history teacher in the New York City schools for twenty years, I found myself frequently wondering how the city's textbooks have gotten so full of errors and liberal hogwash.

The latest textbook we are required to use (no exceptions) in my school's U.S. history courses is *The Americans*, published by McDougal Littell. Every section of this book is replete with errors and omissions. For example, Wilson's moral diplomacy is called "missionary diplomacy." Our only interest in beginning the Spanish-American War was our desire to protect U.S. business interests -- and this contention is expressed with a tone of contempt, as though we were again defending those dirty, filthy, greedy businessmen. The section about Theodore Roosevelt's international affairs involvements does

---

[13] Section originally published at www.americanthinker.com March 25 2012.

not mention the Algeciras Conference, nor does it mention the sending of the "Great White Fleet" around the world. His mediation of the treaty ending the Russo-Japanese War misleadingly states that he became involved thanks to the Japanese, down-playing Roosevelt's initiative in those negotiations. Taft's "dollar diplomacy" is portrayed as a crass attempt to bulwark greedy American bankers in exploiting, for example, Nicaragua. (I had to explain to the students that when a country is bankrupt, no bank or banks will lend that country money. Nobody lends money to anybody without an expectation of being repaid. Therefore, when the banks that agreed to lend money to Nicaragua were given partial ownership of Nicaragua's national railroad, and when the U.S. also went in to collect Nicaraguan customs duties, these actions were a partial hedge against total default by Nicaragua.)

However, I want to focus especially on the textbook's summary of the causes of World War I, used to introduce U.S. entry into and participation in that war. Thousands upon thousands of students in my school and in New York have formed a grossly wrongheaded understanding of the causes of that war.

The textbook lists the four general causes of WWI, and they are in essence the same causes as listed by every textbook I have used for twenty years: nationalism, imperialism, militarism, and the alliance system (some books talk about the "balance of power"). Nationalism is defined as "a devotion to the interests and culture of one's nation." And this nationalism was further complicated by the Balkan ethnic climate, whereby various ethnicities lived within Austria-Hungary but yearned for national independence, or else to be under the (Slavic) Russian influence.

I believe that by calling this configuration "nationalism," the textbook authors are trying to send a left-wing signal against nationalism and patriotism. Is not the left wing, since the days of Trotsky, always claiming to be an international movement rather than a nationalistic one? And have they not tried to identify with so-called minority "nationalisms" as a way of undermining nations like the USA? In short, is not "devotion to the interests and culture of one's nation" a good thing? Yet the left, with its essential anti-Americanism, is always promoting the "nationalism" (sic) of minorities against the claims of patriotism that bind our country together. Would it not make more sense to describe the overreaching nationalism prior to WWI as chauvinism or hyper-nationalism instead? Then our students and populace could be free of guilt for being nationalistic or patriotic.

The term "imperialism" is lifted right out of the Karl Marx playbook. This term draws attention to the inherent economic motive at the center of all national decisions of countries operating within a capitalistic framework. The book says, "For many centuries, European nations had been building empires, slowly extending their economic and political control over various people of the world." We know that "imperialism" is a sub-heading of "historical necessity" for Marxists. Capitalists and capitalistic countries must conquer and exploit as an automatic part of the dialectical process (that is, until the dialectic expands to the point where the capitalists produce the opposition that overthrows capitalism and establishes communism).

Yet the book fails to take into account that conquest of other peoples goes back in history to pre-industrialized societies. Man's urge to dominate, conquer, or even crush his neighbor is deeply rooted in the human psyche and is not a trait of the capitalist mindset per se. That's one of the reasons why early Christianity was so unique -- because it was built on the principle of "love thy neighbor," not "dominate thy neighbor." In fact, there are articles and books blaming the downfall of Rome on Christianity for just this reason. Other reasons for conquest include fame, glory, status, and adventure -- not only for economic gain, as the Marxists would believe.

Thirdly, militarism is cited as an effect of nationalism and imperialism. Yet there is no mention of culture clashes or wars about competing visions of civilization. Rather, all these develop-ments are brought together under a unified leftist-Marxist formula. High school textbooks typically see the arms buildups of Germany and Great Britain as merely an effect of the deep-seated economic competition between these countries. Yet many books have been written about the different visions between Germans and the British of what makes a good society. Many Germans believed that British elevation of the rule of law, of the individual, of parliamentary government, and of the central role of commerce in the life of the country was offensive, and that the Germans had a superior, more militant and romantic view of manly heroism than had the British. Many Germans believed that German efficiency trumped British liberty. Further, the British (and French, for that matter) were far more successful than the Germans in extending their colonial hegemony in foreign lands. Yet this textbook never considers any of these overriding cultural differences, or, one might say, the clash of worldviews.

Lastly, this book (and all other textbooks I have used) refer to the alliance system, or balance of power, as a cause of WWI. The book is ambivalent. On the one hand, the Triple Entente and the Triple Alliance were intense rivals and antagonistic -- but, at the same time, "nations were reluctant to disturb the balance of power," so these same antagonistic alliances also helped keep the peace (for a while). At this point, the textbooks are unwilling to ask the question: "Which of the alliances was truly defensive, and which of the two alliances was more motivated by hostility and aggressive intentions?" Only after WWI was Germany forced to sign the war guilt clause taking responsibility for the war. Yet, as every pacifistic leftist knows, this was quite mean-spirited of the Allies to require of Germany. This was just an expression of that vengeful real-politik spirit of George and Clemenceau, and not of our magnanimous Pres. Wilson. However, if the war guilt clause was in fact a true statement, then it was not the alliance system that caused World War I, but the Triple Alliance of Germany,Austria-Hungary, and the Ottoman Empire that was fundamentally wrong in its intentions and actions.

As we reflect on the above information about textbooks now used in the teaching of U.S. history in New York City and across the nation, we can see that every detail on every page should be recon-sidered, refined, and restored to a greater degree of historical accuracy, and diverted from an underlying leftist slant that permeates the writing of almost every page disseminated.

REVIEW OF *THE RED PENCIL: CONVICTIONS FROM EXPERIENCE IN EDUCATION* BY THEODORE R. SIZER

I first encountered Ted Sizer's views on education in his course on The American School at the Harvard Graduate School of Education. The idea that most surprised me was his desire to model Harvard's role in American education after that taken by Dewey and his disciples who had trained a high number of America's superintendents during an earlier era. He told us that those of us in the M.A. in Teaching program had been selected in part because we would go on to leadership in various schools and school systems, and could effect change. We would carry the "message" of Harvard regarding our respective disciplines and about the running of the schools as a whole. This struck me then, and still does, as an essentially egotistical concept of his role in education. It was more about power than about educational vision. His role as a reformer trying to dominate and change the schools of the country has continued throughout the years.

In his writings, he usually focuses on the negative. There is something so basically flawed about the schools it must be weeded out. Yet, it is hard to pin down exactly what is wrong. Sometimes, along with Robert Coles and others, he seems to opine that there are so many youths who are alienated by the system. When I taught in Dedham High School in Massachusetts years ago, one teen declared that he was "an outlaw." He wanted to get a mobile home and a motorcycle and ride rootlessly around the country "like a rolling stone." Sometimes Sizer writes as though he wants to change the system in order not to lose youths like this one. Other times, he is concerned with the cynicism of the better students, who have learned to play the system to their advantage. They have learned to manipulate the system in order to "succeed," but a true ideal of excellence is missing from their value system, or even a true love of learning.

Sizer is bothered by the bureaucracy, but it's not that there is just too much paperwork or too much micromanagement, or a lack of disciplinary follow through and guts in punishing the guilty. Rather, from reading Sizer's writings we understand that the bureaucracy is a mindset he abhors. It is a mindset of mediocrity and of trying to manage or enclose an educational process that is more exciting and open-ended than is realized. However, by promoting the small schools movement, the urban school districts have only managed to decrease the number of bureaucrats in a given school, not the bureaucratic mentality which abounds more than ever.

In short, he believes that for the past forty-plus years education is not living up to what it could and should be. Yet, he never clearly articulates what it could and should be. Rather, he is inviting us, and all potential fellow reformers, to catch his vision that there is a dynamic and an excellence beyond what we now have, even if the parameters of that dynamic and that excellence cannot be fully enunciated. He's kind of an educated Rodney King..."if we could all just get together, then what a beautiful world it could be." But it ain't a beautiful world although there is beauty in it. A more healthy and robust philosophy is needed to adjust to the wickedness that is out there.

He does not call for implementation of a more moral worldview as did Pestalozzi. He does not promote the adaptation of the individual to democracy as does Dewey. He does not promote radical freedom of the individual like the Summerhill crowd. He does not advocate integration like Martin Luther King, Jr. He does not challenge us to intensify the scientific application of psychology to learning as does Herbart. Nor, does he advocate the arts as a path to wholeness in the educational life of a growing human being like Rudolf Steiner. Since I studied with him in 1963, I do not see articulated positive goals, but only the sense that if one is smart enough and progressive enough then he or she will see how to reform and improve this or that school or school system, because the given is that they all need reform. His "new vision" really is no vision, but only the promise that if you work with him your schools will get better in all kinds of ways. They will be revitalized. In fact, if I were to give a rubric for his ideas, I would say they come under the heading of "revitalizing the schools." However, the rub is that the notion is vague and even mystical. It ultimately depends upon trusting him and those who agree with him.He has good points to make yet lacks overriding substance in terms of goals or purpose.

Lastly, it is worth noting that Sizer is not "above the fray." Though certain of his points might be considered acceptable to conservative or liberal theories of education, he is in the liberal/left camp although not a full blown Marxist. Why can't Johnny read? Answer: The schools are boring, have me-me-me-diocrity as their standard, have untalented administrators and teachers, lack funding, are mired in local values and premises that are invalid and provincial, and have arcane rules that inhibit rather than enhance educational practice. Almost every aspect of pedagogy, administration, testing, discipline, parent-school relations, curriculum, guidance, and legal structure is wrong. Why can't Johnny tell right from wrong? Answer: Pretty much the same as the answer for why Johnny can't read.

Ted Sizer sees very little that is good about education as it has evolved in America. His slant is leftward. His sense that the individual can only be fixed by reforming the whole is ill-conceived and based on many philosophical misassumptions. His sense that the traditional classroom is a place of failed expectations and rampant denial is excessively negative. His hope for America based on his en-visioned educational reforms is futile.

DOES THE DECLARATION OF INDEPENDENCE TELL THE TRUTH?[14]

On July 4th, while most U.S. citizens are contemplating U.S. independence and the Declaration of Independence, I ask myself why, in nineteen years of teaching in the New York public schools, I have not once heard the students gathered to sing in any assembly or forum "America the Beautiful," "God Bless America," or "My Country 'Tis of Thee." The National Anthem has been sung only once a year, at the graduation ceremonies.

This serious omission of patriotic fervor can be attributed to the leftist influence on the school system. Most leftists believe the Declaration of Independence was primarily a document driven by the class interests of the signers. The gentry and economically powerful merchant groups in the U.S. and the aristocratic southern plantation economy joined forces against powerful interests in the mother country that would limit their growth, their

---

[14] First published at www.americanthinker.com July 4 2010.

economic well-being, and their power. Talk about inalienable rights, equality, life, liberty, and the pursuit of happiness were rationalizations for underlying issues of class and status. Charles and Mary Beard set the stage for this analysis, and it has been carried forward by Howard Zinn's People's History of the United States. Are they correct?

First, a caveat: Even if the document were a justification of class interests in part, would that be so wrong? If we have an economic leadership based on wealth amassed through faith, hard work, determination, and intelligence, then is it not just for them to defend that wealth and influence from usurpations by those who would unlawfully take said wealth and influence away from them? The truth of "no taxation without representation" is a valid truth, but it certainly oversimplifies the dynamics behind the Declaration of Independence.

Let us consider one of the more contentious statements of the Declaration:

> "We hold these truths to be self-evident, that all men are created equal, that they are endowed by

their Creator with certain
unalienable Rights, that among
these are Life, Liberty and the
pursuit of Happiness; ..."

John Locke in his treatises on government made
a cogent analysis of the body politic and stressed
that life, liberty and property could best be protected
if the locus of power in the government lay with the
representatives of the people rather than with the
executive -- or in his context, the monarchy. The
signers of the Declaration, aware of the moral am-
biguities of slavery in the American context, deleted
the word "property," and preferred to substitute
"pursuit of happiness." They introduced this
Aristotelian goal in order (1) to acknowledge the
existence of a *summum bonum*, (2) to point to the
unity of happiness and virtue (happiness for
Aristotle was arrived at by strenuous contemplation
and implementation of virtue, and was not, as in our
times, associated with hedonism or with "self-
fulfillment" à la Abraham Maslow), and (3) to
introduce the idea of the newly independent USA as

a land of opportunity, both economically and politically. How can this be offensive?

Although the Declaration was not in one accord with the 17th-century Westminster Shorter Catechism that announced the purpose of life to be "to glorify God and to enjoy Him forever," we can see that the Declaration, by insisting that the values expressed in it are "endowed by their [the people's] Creator," is an echo of the earlier Westminster document. The language suggests to me that the Declaration was deeply rooted in Protestant theology more than in class interests.

What about the self-evidence of the truths claimed in our founding document? This assertion is directly out of the rationalist enlightenment play-book. R. Descartes had affirmed that he could believe only truths that were "clear and distinct." To be clear and distinct, they had to meet the challenge of his method of doubt. If there were any possibility that the truths he perceived could be contingent or could be based on misperception, they would be excluded. Through experience and various other mechanisms, J. Locke's empiricism believed that certainty could be arrived at through experience, science, and intuition.

While these self-evident truths for the signers were not the same as revealed truth as found in Holy Scripture, they are still "endowed" to all men by God the Creator. In theological language, they would be considered part of common grace, whereas for the believing Christian, the Bible comes under special or revealed grace. Thus, the Bible tells us that the rain falls equally on the just and the unjust, and in similar fashion, all men are endowed with the right to life, liberty, and the pursuit of happiness. Almighty God must be assumed, because without Him, how could one explain that all men are so endowed?

As we contemplate our independence as a nation and the exercise of our inalienable rights, as we sing hosannas of gratitude for these blessings, let us remember to also reject all Marxist views that would depreciate the values of the Declaration.

EDUCATION HAS MORPHED INTO INDOCTRINATION

In his amazing philosophical and personal autobiography, Allen West observes that "Over the past thirty years. Public education has gradually morphed into public indoctrination."[15]

Students are gradually coming out of our high schools believing that America is a democracy, not a republic. They are totally unaware of the role Judeo-Christian values based on religious faith in building this country. They typically think that an ever-increasing federal government, an increasing national debt, progressively increasing inflation, and the "government knows best" are the basic principles upon which the country was founded (except that there are certain "unenlightened folks" typically living in rural (implied, backwards) areas who do not want to accept the obvious. The pre-mises of federalism, the rule of law, the centrality of individuals, and the sacredness of an individual's right to his or her property (which comes from John Locke's writings) are downplayed or ignored al-together. Instead, too many teachers provide a narrative for U.S. history of rapacious white males living within a rigid ideology based on class and false religion forcing their ideals on an unsuspecting

---

[15] Allen West, *Guardian of the Republic*, Crown Forum, Div. of Random House New York, 2014, p. 121.

and/or victimized society via sexism, slavery, selfish capitalism, exploitation, homophobia (latent at the founding but more and more apparent as time went on), racism, and – perhaps the greatest sin of all – totally uncool absolute values.

But this educational take in itself becomes a threat to the culture when one considers the bombardment of reinforcing elements in the culture from the entertainment, music, and TV communications. Further, lack of reading because of texting and social networking adds to the effectiveness of the indoctrination in the schools. Except for some wonderful British series like Mr. Selfridge, The Bletchly Circle, Masterpiece Theater, and Downton Abbey, TV caters to the lowest common denominator. Variety shows of yesteryear like the Ed Sullivan Show or The Colgate Comedy Hour or the Patti Page Show have been replaced with competitions among rank amateurs for singing honors on the Voice or American Idol. More competition is on America's Got Talent and Dancing With the Stars (many of the "celebs" are not stars). These shows involve countless millions in a vacuity that is truly amazing. Ads for pharmaceutical products appear that include "death" among the possible side-effects [sic]. Drinking, fashion, marijuana, crime, TGIF gatherings, hanging out, Facebook, Tumblr, MySpace, Twitter, etc. become obsessions that take the minds of the people, especially the high school age citizens, farther and farther away from the serious issues, away from reading, and away from knowing what's what about the ordering of values in society, what makes a good citizen, and how to discriminate between lies told to us by an ever-growing and self-serving government and the true values that make for good governance.

Thus the schools are neglecting logic, neglecting facts, neglecting analysis, neglecting synthesis, and we are moving ineluctably towards the "brave new world" described prophetically by Aldous Huxley in his book of that name. Tie this in with interactive communications like Skype, tracking of individuals via their cell phones, data collection by the IRS, National Security Council, the Affordable Health Care Act, Common Core, and the Bureau of the Census all of which is used to control us, direct us, "help" us, lead us, organize us, and allocate resources (sic), and we have a network or web of control from above (from the software companies working with the federal and state governments [especially the former]) that is truly overpowering and threatening of the very foundation of our liberties. The potential for control, for eliminating privacy, combined with indoctrination that individuality is to be de-valued, should not be underestimated. Joseph Goebbels under the National Socialist Workers Party (NAZI's) was considered the pre-eminent propagandist of his era. But thought control techniques have evolved far beyond mere propaganda, which disseminates false information on a large scale as though it were true.

Today, through advertising techniques, both subliminal and overt, as well as indoctrination in the schools, plus technology becoming controling, and we see an unprecedented threat to individual initiative and individual decision-making. Is it not obvious that if the schools are indoctrinating youth, and if the skills and incentives to be thinking persons who will and can evaluate these attempts at indoctrination are removed by creating passive mindsets, then the indoctrination will go unchallenged. In the wonderful book *Fahrenheit 451* by Ray Bradbury, only a remnant who read (and memorized) books were able to keep alive a resistance to the status quo of ignorance that prevailed in that fictional society.

In one high school in New York, Howard Zinn's widely used Communist textbook, *A Peoples' History of the United States*, is required reading. This book is already a best seller on many of our college campuses, the textbook of choice for the many left wing professors who have taken control of our college humanities courses. In this textbook, America is depicted as having from the beginning victimized large segments of our population as well as the Native Americans. Our greed, racism, and sexism are dominant values used to exploit the population within the U.S. and peoples (especially of color) throughout the world. If there is no one in the schools to challenge the assumptions of the book, and if outside the schools there is little to challenge the assumptions or to encourage the reasoning which would allow the students to challenge these left wing assumptions on their own, then the students will become indoctrinated. And, indeed, many of them are.

Richard Ofshe and Margaret Singer have published some important works on brainwashing strategies of cults. Their classic article on this topic states the following:

During the last decade there has been a dramatic renewal of public and academic interest in the procedures and effects of "coordinated programs of coercive influence and behavior control." That is, programs designed first to induce radical changes in facets of a person's worldview (e.g., beliefs about a political philosophy, scientific theory, psychological theory, ethical philosophy, etc.), and subsequently to generate great conformity to organizationally specified prescriptions for behavior. The combined effects of (1) acceptance of a particular world view, (2) establishment of effective procedures for peer monitoring, including feedback about an individual to the controlling organization, and (3) the use of psychological, social, and material sanctions to influence a target's behavior, can render a person a highly deployable agent of an organization.[16]

The above quotation references changes in the mind control strategies of cultic organizations in our world. "Brainwashing" in China or the USSR 30 years ago, emphasized inducing of radical change in what authors call "extrinsic" or "peripheral" elements of self. Those would include social status, role performance, conformity to societal norms, political and social opinions, taste, etc. But the above go towards inducing changes in one's world-view and "personal aspirations, sexual experience, religious beliefs, estimates of the motivations of others...." These would be considered "central" or "intrinsic" elements of self.

The authors note that education includes both intrinsic and extrinsic elements of self. They go on to wisely suggest that "Schools will perform these functions better if they do not confuse their role with the parental role or with the political role, i.e., they should not become ideological arms of the local political power structure [or, one might add they

[16] http://www.icsahome.com/articles/attacks-on-peripheral-ofshe-and-singer-csj-3-1

should not become arms of the anti-local political power structure, i.e., the leftist or statist ideologues]...."[17] Yet, this is what we have seen in recent years. The schools are no longer operating from a philosophy of *in loco parentis*, especially at the high school level, but, the parents are operating, to coin a term, *in loco educationentis*. The schools are no longer trying to uphold the values of the families who send their kids there, nor are they trying to "Americanize" kids, as in past generations, who may come from immigrant homes. Rather, the schools are calling the shots, and the homes have to go along.

Thus, while Ofshe and Singer are primarily analyzing the dynamics of psychological or religious cults that seek to alter the worldviews of members, we can see the application of their work to our schools and the potential danger of repeated exposure of our youth to the "revisions" of the three categories noted.

Acceptance of a particular worldview: There is a continuous pressure to accept the premises of a socialist-statist-communist-progressive worldview in

---

[17] Ibid.

the high schools, particularly in New York City.

Continuous peer monitoring: collection of data by Common Core (including academic history and social adjustment history) as well as by the Affordable Health Care exchanges leaves considerable room for manipulation of the individual student's intrinsic values (self-image) over the course of many years of education.

Use of psychological, social, and material sanctions to influence a target's behavior: Grades by teachers, questions asked and discussed in class, and feedback from the teacher and fellow students influence a target's behavior. This writer asked students whether they would vote for Romney or Obama in the last Presidential election, and 99% said they would vote for Obama. If one considers that a vote of 60% for a candidate is considered by voting experts to be a landslide victory, then the student vote was far beyond a landslide. The leftward tilt of mind control is already quite apparent. Thus, education is beginning to more and more to resemble a cult in terms of the uniform results that are appearing. With data gathering by Common Core and leftist teachers emboldened by the election of

Pres. Obama, we can expect even more intense pressures to be brought into the classrooms of our country. But, because these pressures are taking place in a public school, because they are not apparently planned by a conspiracy but occur "naturally" (sic), there is no sense that the students are being brainwashed or having their intrinsic, or central, values compromised.

We are told in Ofshe and Singer's landmark article,

An individual immersed in a world in which communication is strictly limited must either remain aware of the difference between private beliefs and permitted public expression or, somehow, come to reconcile public expression with private self. If an environment that permits peer interaction only in terms of certain values and beliefs, it is likely that even a person's statements about what he or she actually values will eventually be molded into the contours of the controlling environment. This leaves the person in the position of surface conformity with perhaps private disagreement.[18]

Students today through the enforced political correctness of the classroom are more and more becoming convinced that they need to keep their private disagreements, if they have them, to themselves.

---

[18] Ibid.

PART FOUR: WHY WOULD A PERSON BECOME A TEACHER?

IMPORTANCE OF MOTIVES FOR CHOOSING A TEACHING CAREER

Do you want to be a teacher? Are you in college and considering a teaching career? Are you considering a mid-life career change? This little book is an attempt to help you understand what is involved with teaching in general, and teaching in an urban setting in particular. This work also includes a chapter on teaching social studies. You should know that there are as many teaching styles as there are people. Some teachers are reserved; others are gregarious, outgoing types. Some speak softly and others loudly. Some are friendly with the students; others are remote and authoritarian. Some are beautiful; others are homely or decrepit.

No one is excluded from teaching; yet, teaching is one of the most noble callings on the face of the earth. In the Holy Bible, Paul tells us that some are called to be preachers, teachers, pastors, prophets and evangelists. Notice, he does not say that some are called to be bankers or lawyers or even physicians! The special, set aside vocations include teaching. Teaching is an activity that not only finds special favor in the sight of God, but is an activity with high responsibilities. To whom much is given, much is expected.

Thus, from the outset it should be understood that a special area of interest for a would-be teacher is MOTIVE. Do you believe that teaching is something that God has really called you to do? Or are you merely bored by the prospect of a nine to five job? Do you wish to lift others to higher levels of wisdom, understanding, and knowledge? Or do you simply like to have the spotlight on you? Are you seeking a self-importance that you do not believe you can achieve in the world of working with adults? Or do you have a vision of the possibilities of influencing the future?

It is very important that you assess the purity and sincerity of your motives. It is important that teaching not be an escape, but a destination!

EXPLANATIONS AND QUESTIONS LEAD TO THE MAIN IDEA

Teachers wear many hats. They are counselors, public speakers, resource persons, facilitators, leaders, actors and actresses, friends, fathers, mothers, uncles, brothers, and cousins. The Number One ability for a teacher to have is the ability to EXPLAIN. Most teaching time is spent explaining. A teacher should be prepared to explain the meaning of concepts, words, ideas, longer texts, and the meaning of life.

Likewise, teachers are explaining the relation of student explanations to the comments of other students and other comments or explanations made by the teacher. Explanations include causation, effects, implications, ramifications, possibilities, contingencies, variables, timing, definitions, descrip-tions, analyses, and analogical reasoning. Explanations are given to clarify, but the expla-nations them-selves may need clarification. A good explanation clarifies, but does not reduce the subject being explained to a level of simplicity whereby the integrity and TRUTH of that subject is lost. The explanation may include raising important questions.

Sometimes good questions are seen as ends in themselves by educators. Or questions are seen as a way of eliciting student participation. However, it is my view that questions should be understood by the teacher as advancing the scope and depth of the explanation. The teacher should have before his or her mind that he or she is GOING SOMEWHERE....

In light of this please consider the following questions:

How would you define...?
How would you describe...?
What are the implications...?
Can you think of any parallels...?
What would happen (would have happened) if...?
To what extent...?

The above are six question formats that are useful in teaching. However, a teacher may ask himself/herself: why am I asking these questions? Do I want to encourage classroom participation? Do I want the students to think? These are certainly valid goals. However, I think the teacher should build step-by-step to the MAIN IDEA of the lesson. He or she should have something to say, a message if you will, about the material and/or about life. That message should be left with the students each day. Dealing with each unit should leave the students with an even bigger message. By the end of the term, the students should get some very big messages like:

THE TRUTH ABOUT HISTORY (ENGLISH, SCIENCE, MATHEMATICS) MUST BE SOUGHT AND FOUND!!

IT'S ESSENTIAL TO KNOW WHAT IS IMPORTANT AND WHAT IS NOT IMPORTANT.

LIFE IS WORTH LIVING.

THE TOOLS FOR INDEPENDENT LEARNING ARE BEING PUT IN MY HANDS.

I AM PART OF A FABULOUS ENTERPRISE OF WORLD-WIDE EDUCATION, AND I CAN CONTRIBUTE!!

KNOWING REALITY IS INCOMPARABLY MORE FASCINATING AND VALUABLE THAN KNOWING FANTASY, VIRTUAL REALITY, OR ADVERTISING HYPE.

WHY DIDN'T YOU LISTEN TO YOUR MOTHER?

Please let me ask you a question: do you ever wonder why you didn't take your mother's advice and become a doctor instead of a teacher? I do. At least in medicine you get definitive results: either the patient dies or he gets off the operating table with a heart transplant and resumes a normal life. Have you noticed that teaching isn't nearly so clear cut? Some people would like to transplant the brain of a bull into the students and call the results "creativity." Bizarre mental experiments are performed on the innocent, and we are left trying to separate the bad results from the good results for decades. You see, one person has the intelligence to sweep a floor, another has intelligence to sketch a flower, and another has the intelligence to create the theory of relativity. Don't start thinking that one of these three is more intelligent than the others. Yep, it's great to be able to explain human differences, ain't it? By the way, my grandmother was a pretty good cook, without using any recipes, and she couldn't speak English either. Take that Julia Child!

RESPECT FOR AUTHORITY HAS COLLAPSED

Background of Today's Student Disrespect

To some degree, self-hatred of Americans for themselves qua Americans had roots as early as the 19th century. Going back to Henry David Thoreau and Ralph Waldo Emerson and the Brook Farm experiment, we see the intellectual elite expressing disgust with "Christian morality" and spirituality, and with the banalities and guilt-ridden excesses of the new American civilization. There were attempts at new communities like Brook Farm and Oneida where different lifestyles might live acceptably within an American society alienated from the goals of those communities' members.

By the 1920's, the expatriate movement led by T.S. Eliot, Henry Miller, and Ernest Hemingway presented us with a vision of disgust with America and with so-called materialistic values that was more encompassing than the Transcendentalists. The expatriates had to get away from the USA entirely. They found those decadent European roots, that the new American civilization eschewed, to be more congenial to their artistic, intellectual, and personal needs. Sexual licentiousness was not looked down upon in Europe as much as in America. To the French, the response was oo-la-la, and a good humored laugh. To the Europeans, even to post-Victorian England, America was prudish and up-tight. "Sin," so real to millions of Americans, had become a concept unattractive to Europeans. D.H. Lawrence and James Joyce sang the joys of coitus; and Sigmund Freud legitimized their desire to throw off the cloak of inhibitions. Henry Miller and Anais Nin rollicked in their self-indulgent artistic play-ground. Ernest Hemingway strutted his machismo lust for death. T.S. Eliot was able to lose himself in an intellectual wonderland, with excitement in his own mind rather than in the superficialities of a banal and loveless society. The expatriate disgust with American values in the 1920's, with morality in particular, and with enjoyment of the material goods of our society, was somewhat obliterated by the Great Depression in the 1930's. At that time, even the writers and artists wanted help from the govern-ment to get some of those same material goods that they had so disparaged and taken for granted in the 1920's.

After WWII, the Beatniks writhed in their bookstores and coffee shops, in the subways, and in their filthy crash pads, screaming with pain in the works of Jack Kerouac, William Burroughs, Allen Ginsberg, and Lawrence Ferlinghetti that the American eagle should spread its wings and fly right. Ginsberg gave the finger to Judeo-Christian morality with defiant poems justifying his pederasty, homosexuality, defecation in public places, and other obscenities. Others romanticized their alcoholism and heroin addiction, identifying themselves with Poe, Baudelaire, and Coleridge. Their self-romanticization combined with aggressive condemnation of all non-degenerates set the stage for the Hippie movement, and later for the institutionalization of disrespect that resulted from the civil rights movement and the anti-War movement.

The beatniks lacked the grace of the expatriates; they did not have the grace to leave the country. Instead, they heaped their vitriol and hot ashes of contempt upon America. They insisted that they were making a statement by their dirtiness and degeneracy. Their tone was not the tone of criticism of the culture as was the tone of the Transcendentalists

125 years before. Rather, their tone was one of accusation and of overpowering hatred and disgust for the U.S.A. The title of Ginsberg's masterwork – *Howl* – sums up the underlying impulse and reaction of the "Beats." Ginsberg lay on a dirty bed in India, and compared himself to Jesus Christ. What a cowardly and blasphemous liar!

The "howl" was in the hearts of the Beatniks, and is still there in the hearts of our adolescents and of the country's leadership. The beatniks reached a fever pitch of spiritual and psychic pain. They were the accusers of society. Yet, they were not main-stream. Very few people heard of them. They made no dent in the American consciousness. Rather, another mass movement, more powerful than any before, would light up the dark side of the American consciousness, would turn a moral and decent people gradually away from Judeo-Christian values in the direction of the powder-puff morality and incon-sequential thinking we find today. That movement was rock 'n roll. Doo-wop, hard rock, and MTV were stages in rising mindlessness and cacophony. Sounds took precedence over songs with their harmonious melodies and lovely lyrics. Sexuality devoid of romance was placed at the center of experience. Gradually electronic sounds began to replace instruments. Youthful high spirits were gradually replaced with a drug-fueled bedlam masquerading as "music." Today we have rap music and trap music to accompany the buzz of the latest high.

This entire history of disaffection with America converged in the 1960's with opposition to the Vietnam War. Radical hate groups emerged along with widespread popular dissent from the War and perception of the U.S. as "bad guys" rather than "good guys" in a large segment of the population.

Opposition to the Vietnam War – especially with the youth of America taking to the streets and rioting on the campuses -- was an important step in the collapse of respect for authority. This was reinforced by the drug culture that was expanding exponentially at that time via the Hippie and Yippie movements, and the leadership of immoral hucksters and druggies of the "new age" Richard Alpert (Baba Ram Das), Timothy Leary, Abbie Hoffman, and Jerry Rubin. Violent domestic terrorist groups also emerged such as the Weathermen and the Black Panthers, led by

Huey Newton, Bobby Seale, and Eldredge Cleaver, and to a lesser degree the Student Non-Violent Coordinating Committee led by Stokeley Carmichael and H. Rap Brown. We also saw the destructive work of the Berkeley Free Speech Movement led by Mario Savio combined with the Communists led by Angela Davis.

The Vietnam War gave a kind of moral authority or justification for civil disobedience and violent confrontation. If the students were merely rioting and carrying on because they were drunk after a football game, or high on drugs, then society would clearly have condemned their actions, and those involved might have in a short time seen the error of their ways. But there was a veneer of righteousness in those actions which obscured the significance of the antisocial meaning and wantonness of those demonstrations.

When the U.S. pulled out of Vietnam many of those students felt they had "won," but did they really win? How can a free country "win" when it gives up one of its allies to generations of bondage and degradation? Where was peace? In fact, the U.S. pullout in Vietnam not only harmed the people of the region, but contributed to the prolongation of the Cold War and the arms race. The communist takeover of South Vietnam, Laos, and the Cambodian "killing fields" showed that the domino theory was, in part, correct as the war hawks had been asserting in opposition to the peaceniks or "doves." My heart broke over the plight of the Vietnamese boat people who became part of that vast worldwide population of displaced persons living in utter destitution in refugee camps. Yes, some of our behavior in Vietnam was despicable, but the foul order of communism still reeks in those lands, and degradation is their lot to this very day.

Our loss not only caused our allies to lose faith in us, but the American people lost a lot of faith in its leadership, both Democratic and Republican, to properly prosecute a defense of liberty once under-taken. The foul-mouthed, irresponsible demon-strators seemed to win the day after all, and legi-timate government seemed to have failed. This failure made a deep impression in the psyches of the people. The corrupt and decadent voices against the system were elevated to a new plateau of respect, and America's official leadership was demoted to a lower level of respect, that has since become full-blown cynicism and disrespect.

The society that saved democracy from the monarchism and tyrannical Germans in WWI, and from the demonic overlords of fascism in WWII, became perceived as the society that was murdering innocent Asian women and children and depriving underdogs of their rightful claims for national self-determination. During the Vietnam War, America's national self-image shifted from good, even messianic, to that of being selfish, cruel, and wanton.

Vietnam was an expression of our failed policy of containment. This policy had begun under Truman and was first demonstrated by our failure to rescue East Europe from the grip of Stalinism, and then in Korea. Kennan's policy of containment, rather than a policy of liberation for lands enslaved by communism, established the Cold War as a necessity, prevented the U.S. from being the champion of democracy and human rights that it always had been, and, in its ultimate failure in Vietnam, led to the collapse of respect for American leadership and culture that we are facing today.

Had MacArthur been allowed to invade and bomb Manchuria during the Korean War, as he wished to do, we would not have had World War III as Truman feared, and the Chinese and Soviets would not have been emboldened to provide the support they did in Vietnam. Further, as soon as we learned the Soviets had detonated their first atomic bomb, we should have devastated their nuclear plant, just as Israel would later attack the bomb-making facility of Iraq.

Don't you see it? We are still following containment in Cuba with our "economic sanctions," and we are still following containment in Korea with our troops still enforcing the static and unacceptable 38th parallel. Impasse and failure have been the keynotes of U.S. foreign and military policy since the end of WWII. We have avoided WWIII by appeasing the enemy (communism) to a point where communism has taken root in our own country. We don't know what we stand for as a country, and our righteousness is being dismantled from within. Again, communism without the word "communism" has crept through the land like a fog encroaching from the ocean. It's neo-communism, neo-fascism, new new left, neo-nihilism, neo-relativism….neo-, neo-,neo- ….updating of totalitarian attacks on our culture's virtues and values, on the pursuit of happiness, on life, on personal responsibility, on hope for the future, on stability and permanence, on law (lawyers are replacing law)….

Students had been striking against their educational institutions during the Vietnam War. Their chants in the high schools and on the campuses were "hell no, we won't go." When the U.S. withdrew in abject defeat from Vietnam, the protests stopped (actually, the end of protests can be dated from the shooting of students at Kent State by the Ohio National Guard). But the organic unity of the generations in the U.S. -- between young, middle-aged, and old -- was severed irrevocably. A sense of trust and connection had been broken. No longer would students be coming into class, opening their notebooks, and listening attentively to their teachers (in some schools there had already been a breakdown to some degree before Vietnam).

Now the students were coming in and too many were threatening their teachers' persons, stealing teachers' moneys, telling the teachers to get f----d, spitting at teachers, throwing erasers and wads of papers at teachers, tossing chairs over, walking out of class, walking around the class, yelling across the room, banging on their desks, calling out to their teachers "hey dude," never doing any homework, cutting frequently, slashing each other in the hallways, bringing sharpened toothbrushes to school, having sex in the stairwells and closets, shooting up the schools and committing mass homicides, setting fire to schools, setting off false alarms requiring a fleet of fire trucks to rush to schools, hitting on female teachers, refusing to sit in assigned seats, arguing back and insisting ("getting in the faces" of their teachers). At Hellhole High one of our students was shot in the leg after school, and the event was so commonplace, it was not even reported in the newspapers. In short, chaos or near chaos is reigning in so many high schools (and even lower grades), but this disrespect is never discussed frankly in any education courses. This disrespect is clearly a post-Vietnam phenomenon – after that debacle, extreme misbehavior became the norm. One high school Dean told this writer that in his previous school he and his fellow Dean had to dodge home-made bombs that were thrown at them in the stairwells.

The collapse of respect for each other and the attack on respect for authority is taking us into a dark, dark place. We are on a path of doom. Society is on a path to hell.

Testing Chaos Grips Public Schools[19]

New York State has recently acknowledged statistics that show that 75% of New York State students graduate high school, but only 35% of that number is "college-ready." Similar statistics are noted in many states. What is this alarming disconnect leading to? NY State will begin requiring more difficult Regents exams for its high school freshmen and juniors. (The Regents are exams in New York State where students statewide demonstrate the attainment of minimum competencies in the subjects tested.) This move is another giant step into whirling chaos occasioned by the adjustment and readjustment of tests and test scoring.

---

[19] First appeared at www.americanthinker.com August 25, 2013.

Starting next year with the English and Algebra 1 exams, more difficult exams will be put in place. It is assumed that with more difficult exams, schools and teachers will be forced to have higher expectations and teach more demanding courses. However, the question of what a "more difficult test" will actually test is still up for grabs. And one must also ask if more difficult courses will lead to more learning or only to more failures. Putting aside the dubious value of a rubric like "college-ready," one can see the collapse that has emerged in terms of establishing "standards" for students, and in turn using standardized test scores to evaluate teachers (up to 40% of their evaluation in New York).

Let's look at the history. The original Regents exams of 60-70 years ago were at one point in time broken into two exams -- an easier RCT and a Regents exam. Then scoring adjustments were made to both of these to make passing easier. In addition, scrubbing of grades (rereading low-score essay questions with a view to raising the scores) became standard practice, and the scope of scrubbing was widened. Further, this writer was witness at one school to the erasing of grades and substituting of higher grades on a regular basis year after year (which erasing was reported, but to no avail).

Then the questions were made easier as the rate of passing was still too low to satisfy the politicians. At the point that the questions were made easier, a large number of tenured teachers at Brooklyn Tech HS in New York City, a special high school for gifted students, sent a letter of complaint to the New York Board of Regents detailing what was wrong with the new questions in the global history and U.S. history exams and complaining that the new format represented an unacceptable lowering of standards. The Board of Regents did not even have the courtesy to reply to the letter.

At the same time as questions were changed, scoring strategies changed again -- for example, in social studies. In the multiple-choice questions (50 in all), each question correctly answered is not weighted equally. The first 30 questions answered correctly get more weight than each subsequent question. This is to make it easier to pass the exam but less easy to get higher and higher scores.

Throughout all those years, it was regularly reported in the press that the Regents grades were well below those of the NAEP (National Assessment of Educational Progress), although no high school students in New York City were ever required to take the NAEP standardized tests. Then, in an attempt to end scrubbing, the DOE decided not to have teachers from the same high school grade their students' Regents exams, but shipped those students' exams to other high schools for grading under more controlled circumstances. Also, during the past ten years, the RCTs were eliminated, and the Regents were made easier, supposedly somewhere between the level of difficulty of the previous RCTs and that of the previous Regents.

We have a picture of continuous readjustment of test difficulty and test grading. Easier tests with harder grading, harder tests with easier grading, easier tests with easier grading, and harder tests with harder grading.

Not only is this a chaos of adjustment and readjustment, but one must wonder if the questions on the tests were properly normed. Test questions are required to be piloted over a number of real-time test-taking situations in order to have the answers evaluated statistically for their reliability for use in a larger population. With the frequency of changes in test "difficulty" and test-grading, one can only wonder if the proper procedures for standardized test-creation were followed.

Now, add one additional ingredient: evaluating teachers on the basis of these test results. Does it make sense? You will not only have the chaos of not knowing whether the questions and answering parameters are fair, rational, or based on a proper standard of what is in fact a standard, but then they will be factoring in and adjusting scores for such variables as student history of scores on standardized tests (including results of tests where the tests and scoring were themselves not standardized), student socio-economic levels, student races, and possibly student attendance and lateness records.

Upshot: from beginning to end, we no longer can know what a student in a given subject at a given grade should know. We cannot determine if an individual student is or is not college-ready based on said tests. We are losing sight of or have lost sight of the purpose and goals of a high school education as far as knowledge and related competencies go, and instead of becoming more objective and "scientific," we, more than ever, are flying by personal opinion -- also known as "the seat of our pants."

TEACHERS' RIGHTS

There is much more to "teachers' rights" than mere job security as has sometimes been suggested by certain politicians or journalist critics. Teachers' rights are deeply connected via academic freedom to our ability to have a climate of independent (free) thought in the classroom. Critical thinking or "higher order thinking" cannot exist without academic freedom. Many skills can be taught without academic freedom, yes, but the true purpose of education in a democratic society will be lost once academic freedom is taken out of the classroom. Teachers' rights, including salary, job security, freedom from harassment, limitations on teaching loads, etc. are inextricably tied to and intertwined with academic freedom. Ideas for change and improvement must always be weighed against impact on academic freedom. Any attack on this whether from ideologists of the left or right or from technocratic social engineers should be resisted by teachers. Teaching is almost synonymous with freedom. No new educational theory can change that.

Yet, we as a society have a problem. The majority of teachers, and the overwhelming majority of teachers in our most populous urban school districts, are liberal/left/Communistic in their personal, social, and political philosophies of life and of education. Further, the school and the profession is totally professionalized in the sense that the school, as a team of experts, believes that the parents have little to contribute to the actual education of their children. (I'm tempted to make a joke that teachers no longer see themselves as *in loco parentis*, but are just "loco." However, I shall refrain from making this corny joke.) The teachers, sometimes correctly, see themselves as early childhood specialists or specialists in teaching reading skills, or, at the high school level, as subject matter experts who are committed to communicating a complex body of knowledge to the students. Both groups of teachers ask themselves: what can parents ultimately contribute to the sophisticated tasks that education has become? However, at the same time, parents are voters, and so the City of New York particularly has a public relations strategy to involve (sic) parents. Mostly it's a bogus outreach, and often it is failed.

It is bogus because the School Leadership Teams that are constituted at each school to give parents a voice are burdened with so many rules and bureaucratic requirements that, over time, parents are treated as though they are volunteer employees of the Department of Education. PTA meetings are sparsely attended. When I taught in one of the academy schools into which Hellhole High was created, we had 675 students, and on PTA night, I was the only teacher present along with three parents and the principal – Mrs. U.N. Qualified. At another high school where I taught for 15 years, a school with many gifted students, meetings with parents rarely discussed educational issues, but were very intent on fundraising as the parents tended to be more upscale. However, the school had a $25 million per year budget, so it is this writer's opinion that money was the least of its problems.

Although teachers are covered by a rule that they are not allowed to proselytize for any religion, political ideology, or political candidate in the classroom, this rule is routinely ignored. Teachers are strongly expressing their views on a wide range of political and social issues, and those positions typically are variations of leftist positions. However, some teachers go so far as to even distribute communist literature, or excerpt many pages from leftist textbooks not even on the approved list. When I first came to the school for the gifted – HSFALOAK – High School for Advanced Learning of All Knowledge – and met with the teachers of U.S. History to coordinate strategies for teaching the subject, many members of the committee congratulated each other for not using the textbooks, but instead photocopying large segments of Howard Zinn's *Peoples' History of the United States* for student use. When I told the group that Prof. Zinn (now deceased) was a self-proclaimed communist, and that the citizens whom he called "the people" left out large segments of the population, my colleagues jumped down my throat. "What do you know?" they shrieked. "Have you ever published anything? Every teacher has a bias that he or she is sharing anyhow – we're just more honest and announce our 'bias' to the students." I was blasted, but I remained steadfast. "Teaching should be balanced, and should not be in the service of ideology," I insisted.

Concerned citizens must also consider the educational distortions caused by the existing regimen of standardized tests. Citywide, over a 20+ year period of my service, there was an accelerated emphasis upon standardized testing as though this would assure student progress and teacher accountability. New York State, for decades, has had a series of Regents Examinations to test for student competencies in high schools in a variety of subjects. In recent years, there have been many moves, spurred by the No Child Left Behind legislation enacted during President Bush's presidency, to evaluate teachers based on student scores on those tests. Further, in recent years at HSFALOAK (High School for Advanced Learning of All Knowledge) and many other high schools, these standardized results are being used as 10% or as much as 20% of a student's final grade. This means that the classroom becomes increasingly oriented towards passing this test.

The student as a prescient being who can critically evaluate his or her options, and think through issues, is now increasingly perceived as a test taking robot who can jump through qualifying hoops of Regents. In short, by intensely limiting the goal(s) of education, the idea is to increase the passing and the graduation rates to present evidence of "success" to the citizens and to the Federal Government, source of funding largesse. Likewise students are increasingly being pressured and forced into AP classes even though they are emotionally and intellectually not ready for the demands of those courses. Thus, for the first time in years, students in AP courses are failing those courses or getting C's and D's. However, now, accompanying the forcing into AP, are pressures upon teachers to pass the laggards and those who simply cannot do the work, especially if they are "trying." Also, AP teachers have told me that the AP exams being devised by the College Board are easier today than they were ten years ago. So there is a collusion between the College Board (despite its stellar reputation for many years) and the exploitative school systems that are trying to give the impression of upgrading more and more students.

Further, at the high school level, with the coming of the Internet, more and more students are buying papers and book reports online, or copying whole sections from the worldwide web without caring about research integrity. Stealing ideas without acknowledging their source is common-place, and largely ignored by the New York City public schools. Even a fallible program like www.turniton.com is not supported for use by the teachers in the school system. Because of the ease of copying and lack of integrity of the research, many teachers have abandoned the research paper. Even the gifted students have trouble understanding the methods and philosophy behind citations and writing an authentic paper. To many students, these types of demands by teachers are just part of the uptight system that is putting meaningless obstacles in their path. In my judgment, schools being run by the likes of Mr. Nelson Deceit and Mrs. U. N. Qualified no longer have the moral and ethical leadership that would allow for a consistent case against cheating and plagiarism manifesting. Mrs. Newthoughts would routinely lie about the attendance of her school because the position of her superiors was that if she is doing a good job, then students will not be truant from school. Since truancy continued at a high level when she took over, she inflated attendance figures in order to get a higher rating for herself and the school. She has since retired from education as have Mr. Deceit and Mrs. Qualified.

So, what do we have? Academic freedom that must be protected. But, at the same time, teachers are abusing academic freedom to promote leftist ideologies or, at the very least, leftist positions on a wide range of issues, and educational practices that de-emphasize independent thinking by the students. Lack of integrity in school management, and in the class-room is becoming the norm, and supervisors, often with a liberal-left bias, look the other way even though there are rules against political or religious proselytizing. A host of malpractices and mis-assumptions are in play.

Yet, it's all reinforced by a decline in the family, millions of parents who can't be bothered or don't want to be bothered with their kids, and an ignorance, especially at the high school level, that is growing geometrically. The parents are not reading, but many high school teachers, even at HSFALOAK rarely read a book, and very few ever discuss a book in their day-to-day conversation. Why be bothered reading? In a pre-programmed environment where real love of learning is devalued, where standardized tests are king, where teacher initiative is stifled, where disorder reigns, where student-centered strategies are advocated ad nauseum, why bother learning and growing as a teacher? Just enact the politically correct, liberal-leftist idea that the only relevant socio-political ideal is equality, and that with equality, justice and a perfect world will follow. If you operate within the context of this type of intellectual, spiritual, and emotional stagnation, you will not be challenged, and will pass the test of ideological purity and acceptability. Who would not just go into survival mode and hold steadfast and do what is required and easy for survival in an ***anti-educational*** environment? Reading more books might lead teachers to re-think some of their assumptions…at least if they read more widely. The reading habit and a concomitant openness to new ideas is needed for our teachers, not only for personal growth but for instilling a sense of purpose into teaching and a love of learning into the students. Likewise, the parents need to take a deep breath and start reading as well.

Another friend of mine had a principal who can be described as a hands-on principal with a hands-off philosophy. He would rarely have a conversation with individual teachers, and rarely leave the first floor. His method was that of non-listening. Rather, he had to dominate every conversation and talk about what he was doing. He always had to know more than the people he was talking with. He would often say, "I'm open to different views" on this or that, but as soon as one heard him say that, one could be confident that his mind was made up, and some new policy or program was being rammed down our throats. He went so far as to announce on three different occasions that if teachers did not clean out their lockers before the summer, he would authorize the destruction of all their stored papers, materials, equipment, models, etc. It's like a governor telling people if you don't evacuate before the bad storm comes, I will come with bulldozers and knock your house down.

Further, when these announcements were made, no time was given to take the stuff out (some teachers have been accumulating stuff for teaching for 10-20 years), and the crews started coming in and throwing out not only teaching stuff but photos of wives and children of the teachers, and other personal possessions. Because of tremendous teacher push-back, he had to cease the search-and-destroy operation three times.

In addition, my friend's principal was a bully. He began persecuting the older teachers as part of the Department of Education's war on high seniority teachers in an effort to save money, even if they, especially in a school for the gifted, were doing highly specialized and difficult work that few educators can accomplish. As soon as the teachers organized themselves together, and threatened a lawsuit through the Office of Employment Opportunity that helps victims of age discrimination, this principal would (temporarily) retreat, and only gave one unsatisfactory instead of the numerous unsatisfactory ratings that seemed to be on the original agenda. One of the teachers on the hit list, a respectable gentleman, not a leftist by the way, had his teaching observed while he was giving a test. He was criticized for reprimanding two students who arrived late for the exam!

A LETTER TO A STUDENT EXPLAINING THE GRADE GIVEN FOR A RESEARCH PAPER IN SOCIAL STUDIES

Here's a principle for teachers and would-be teachers: strive for excellence, and do not state that the mediocre is excellent. The letter follows:
Dear R.S.

You have requested a clearer explanation of your grade of 77 in your research paper. I believe my comments are extensive, and express the shortcomings of the paper. Nonetheless, I will further refine my observations if that will help.

The following are problem areas:
1.Unity: A successful paper must express one thesis -- one idea, if you will -- although there may be sub-theses. The main thesis and the sub-theses must be clearly expressed.

Your paper is not written in support of a thesis, one thesis, which runs from beginning to end. Your final sentence ("In the next 100-500 years a rebirth of the family is essential to the psychological, social, and emotional improvement and benefit of man.") might have been your thesis had it come at the beginning. If you had stated that at the beginning, your research would have had to show that the family had declined (1) psychologically, (2) socially, and (3) emotionally to a point where it is dysfunctional. You also would have had to define your terms, because it is not clear to me, nor would it be to any thoughtful reader, what the difference is between "psychologically" and "emotionally." Also, you would have had to show why such a "rebirth" is "essential" since there are certainly many (although I am not one of them) who believe that the family is outmoded and should not be "reborn."

You have not shown any evidence to prove the decline of the family, let alone a demise which requires a rebirth.

2. Coherence : Transitional statements and explanations tying all parts of a paper together are required for a successful paper.

Your paper is divided into roughly four sections.
There are no transitional sentences or paragraphs
between these four sections explaining the
relationship among and between them. There is no
explanation of why these four sections were chosen.
There is no explanation at the end of any section
telling the reader how that section applies to what
came before or sets the stage for what follows in the
paper.

3. Research: A successful research paper should
provide information from secondary and primary
sources which advance the thesis and reveal ideas
and facts which otherwise could not be known.
Further, a research paper should be answering
questions as it moves along -- Why? How? To what
extent? The research paper writer should, as much
as possible, clearly state the questions that are
driving him or her. Also, he or she should anticipate
the questions and thinking of the reader: for
example, having read this, what will the thoughtful
reader wish to know or what objections will that
reader raise to what has been said? Thus, there
needs to be depth and complexity of treatment. Also,

the information provided should be accurately and honestly referenced.

1)As my comments indicated: you have not sufficiently provided references especially on pages 1 and 2.

2)It is not clear what questions either in your mind or in the reader's mind are being answered by the information provided.

3)The instructions provided for use of only one reference from an encyclopedia, but you have two.

4)You have no research in books or articles that have any analysis or conceptualization of issues pertaining to the family. This is the key weakness of the paper. There are no issues presented and no analysis or conceptualization presented either by you in the form of commentary or in the materials which you brought into the paper.

Thus, each section of your paper needs a much more complex treatment. The paper in each of its parts and altogether does not have sufficient depth of treatment.

4. Writing. A good research paper should show concern for the expository (prose) style in which it is

written.   I find your writing style to be above average in terms of vocabulary, clarity, and sense of continuity, as well as your grammar and punctuation. Because of your strengths in this area, your research paper received a significantly higher grade than it would have based only on unity, coherence, and research.

I know you are disappointed, but I cannot find any basis for raising the grade.

Sincerely,

Mr. Ludwig

PART FIVE: SUGGESTIONS TO FOLLOW + PRAYER = HOPE

IS THERE SUCH A THING AS APPROPRIATE DRESS FOR SCHOOL?

The following would of course have to be edited by the administration and the parents of individual high schools, but I think it is at least a starting point for discussion. The slovenly and revealing attire of many of our students has been noted, but little has been done to mobilize for change. If we want to keep individuality in clothing, and not go to uniforms, we need to do a much better job of communicating to students what is and is not desirable.

Dressing for School. It is important that student attire be in keeping with the educational purpose of high school. We are striving to maintain a tone of hard work, order, and seriousness, within a context of sociability. While we do not have a dress code, we encourage all students to follow these rules for attire. If there is cooperation with these goals, it will not be necessary for us to establish a formal dress code. As you know, many schools in New York and throughout the country have opted to go for a formal dress code or uniforms. That is the trend. However, teachers, parents, and the administration much prefer to allow for individual latitude within the bounds of modesty and decorum than to establish the uniformity of a dress code. Teachers have been encouraged to refer students on a case-by-case basis to persons designated by the authority of the principal to evaluate their attire if not in keeping with these rules.

1.   Students should wear comfortable, light clothing in the warm weather that should be fitted proportionately to their size and shape. The wearing of underwear as well as clothes is also deemed to be normal attire.

2.   The following attire may become a cause for concern: halter tops, tank tops, sleeveless undershirts, see-through clothing (top or bottom), shorts that do not extend to the top of the knee, spandex clothes, wearing underwear without clothing on top, or purposely displaying one's underwear. Further, clothing that is unduly tight or unduly low cut may be a cause for concern. Bare midriff is not allowed.

3.   Male students are not to be allowed for any reason to walk in the halls with no shirt or undershirt.

4.   Wearing of jewelry (chains in particular) may be deemed excessive as well as display of "colors" or symbols associated with any gangs.

5.   Do-rags, hats, bandanas, scarves, visors, sweatbands, and all headgear not specified as required for religious purposes are not allowed for both males and females.

BEING, PURPOSE, AND WORLDVIEW: TOWARDS A PHILOSOPHY OF EDUCATION

There is a great deal of confusion today about what is a philosophy of education. A philosophy of education cannot be separated from ontology, for there must be a conception of *being*. A philosophy of education cannot be separated from teleology, for there must be a conception of *purpose*. Lastly, a philosophy of education cannot be separated from cosmology, for there must be a conception of *man's place in the universe*.

Being

1. The individual is an end in himself or herself. But the individual is not to be conceived only in terms of an *en-soi* and *pour-soi* as the existential philosopher Jean-Paul Sartre proposed.[20] For him, absolute freedom to be is the central aspect of the autonomous individual. This aspect of existence is then allied in the modern mindset with Abraham Maslow's hierarchy of values.[21] In this hierarchy, the topmost point of the pyramid is self-actualization. Hence, man uses his or her absolute freedom (Sartre) to attain/maximize actualization.

   Rather, ultimate freedom (which is the underlying belief of the public education system) should be seen as a second level of being. Sartre and Maslow have relevance, but that relevance must be subsumed under theological categories if one is to fully grasp one's place in the universe. All humans were created in the image of God.

---

[20] En-soi is the individual in himself or herself, a fundamental identity based upon his/her absolute freedom. The pour-soi is moving through time and space, becoming if you will, through a range of circumstances and personal choices. For a deep and interesting explanation of these concepts and of absolute freedom as the keystone of Being, see Jean Paul Sartre, *Being and Nothingness* (trans. Hazel Barnes), Washington Square Press, 1993.

[21] Abraham Maslow, *A Theory of Human Motivation*, Martino Fine Books, 2013 (reprint of 1943 edition) as well as Abraham Maslow, *Towards A Psychology of Being*, Sublime Books, 2014.

More important in the construction of a true identity for humankind is the role of the psyche or soul, fallen yet redeemable. In the soul lies the eternal life of the individual, and the demands Almighty God makes upon the individual must be factored in first and foremost. Directly related to the soul is the conscience which supplies us with an inner sense of right and wrong, but if the conscience is not to be manipulated and led astray (it is inborn but not absolute), it must be modified and held to more objective standards of right and wrong that are provided by Judeo-Christian values – values that are thousands of years old, supported by Holy Scripture, and that are edified by prayer, fasting, and supplication to a holy God.

Our precious young people do not exist to be economic units of production as under communism, but have God-given rights to pursue their happiness (including vocation) as they see fit. Thus, my philosophy of being is definitely identified with enlightenment and post-enlightenment ideas about the existence of natural rights, free will, and liberty as essential for the growth of humankind. But the link with Western religion must be maintained in order to stabilize us, and sustain our being as an immortal gift to be used wisely. We are not only free, not only moral, not only seeking happiness, but doing all this within a context of God's love and His requirements.

2. Everyone has a right to the best possible education. Alexis DeToqueville's emphasis on producing a thoughtful, informed citizenry is crucial if we are to avoid the number one pitfall of democracy recognized since Aristotle: the tyranny of the majority. Each individual must have sufficient intellectual tools as well as information to make informed decisions about his everyday life in the political and economic realms.

3. You cannot know yourself without knowing about your history and the social dynamics in which you operate. Thus, the humanities, with history, philosophy, and [English] language, are essential for the individual to form a complete picture of himself.

4. The great design of history should be revealed in high school as it is the time when the mind is sufficiently mature to begin to comprehend the

development and significance of events that may be remote in time and space. History is a study of the rise and fall of civilizations, of immense power struggles, of yearning and work for economic well-being, of mankind's spiritual and artistic aspirations, and of continuous face-offs between good and evil (with a lot of moral gray areas).

5. The social studies movement began as a way of orienting the growing person to having citizenship virtues; however, the classical emphasis on "great books" which marked late 19th century education (before mass education became the norm) should be acknowledged as having a lot merit. It is important that some of the elevated ideas and noble intents of the great world literature continued to be recognized in our more egalitarian and technologically advanced society.

Purpose

1. Students who are going on to higher education must be prepared for success in entering the college or university of their choice, and doing well at that institution. High school is a crucial building block in developing good attitudes,

effective study habits, as well as the highest level skills to deal with the challenges of college life. We have to help our students, but at the same time, if there is too much spoon feeding, they may not develop the independence necessary to study in college. I believe that emphasis on research builds the right outlook in the college bound.

2. For those not bound for college as well as for the college bound, it is important to develop a work ethic. Sometimes the work ethic has been referred to as the Protestant work ethic because of the high value placed upon work by our Puritan forebears. However, it is not necessary to consider hard work as the province of some religious tradition. Rather, it is the basis for accomplishment and essential for satisfaction in life.

The wonders of technology have opened many new windows of opportunity (no pun intended), but one of the downsides of this is the "push button mentality" of many young people. It is my view, however, that deferred gratification is necessary for a successful life and for a civilized society. Immediate gratification leads to short-sightedness, excessive emphasis on "fun," laxity in interpersonal relations ("que sera sera"), and even much crime can be traced to this underlying wrong desire. Of course, immediate gratification has a place in society -- for it is connected with spontaneity and an ability to be a bit carefree, not weighted down with worries about the future. But when it goes too far, as is often the case with youth today, then a corrective balance in favor of hard work must be applied.

3. While extra-curricular activities and socializing are important in developing the whole person and leadership aspects of reality (as well as part-time jobs which for some students are a necessity), the school's focus at the high school level should primarily be on studying and mastering the academic requirements. There is ultimately a deeper satisfaction in getting that "85" rather than a "75" or "70," and true self-worth will be more enhanced this way than by being involved with non-academic activities. The truth is that a lot of young people are neglecting their studies because

they are falling into habits of lonely lounging around, or "hanging out" or playing too many video games and getting involved in negative activities via the internet.

4. Internet material must be studied, analyzed, and placed within a proper context just as if it had come out of a book. In other words, the easy part of Internet access to information should not be thought of as a substitute for the work one must do once one has that information. No matter how much computer or specialized engineering knowledge has been applied to build a bridge, it still takes time and a lot of hard work to build that *real* [not virtual] bridge. The computer is a sophisticated tool, and not an end in itself.

5. A very difficult intangible to inculcate in the student is caring, a sense that he or she should wish to make a contribution to society and lead a productive life. Here, the teacher must be a role model, an example, of a right thinking, positive, action person who wants to do right by others, and to use his or her knowledge to help others, not

dominate others. There is an element of self-lessness which needs to be adapted to our otherwise competitive, and, yes, selfish world. We are all guilty of wanting things for ourselves too much, but I am convinced that some people are more on the giving side than on the taking side. That spirit of giving of oneself is an over-riding value or virtue, if you will, that will serve young people well as they move into their [adult] future.

One's Place In the Universe

The Judeo-Christian worldview establishes clearly that we are living in a God-centered universe. Man is not at the center, and therefore self cannot be. Thus, the "-isms" of our time must be consciously rejected by this philosophy of education, including Marxism, existentialism, pragmatism, hedonism, materialism, and atheism.

♦ Marxism places undo emphasis upon economics and determinism. We are not determined by our class, nor is history driven by a dialectical process leading inevitably towards a "withering away of the state" as Marx predicted. Rather, we are governed by moral absolutes, a God who rules our destiny as individuals and collectively, and by love, not material relations.

♦ Existentialism places too much emphasis upon the circumstances in which man finds himself, and is, ultimately, both too passive and ungodly. Existence does not precede essence. Humanity is created in the image of God. Every person is born with a soul and a conscience. The opportunity to deepen one's relationship with the Almighty is there for all people. All of humanity is sinful, but redemption is possible. The ultimate destiny for all of humanity is governed by supernatural moves and decisions of God beyond our control or understanding. Yet, within the context of these first priorities, education affords us a plenitude of opportunities to grow and to exercise a true freedom. The free agency of man and the moral dimension of life are downplayed in existential literature, particularly the writings of the existential atheists like Sartre and Camus. The idea of "thrown-ness" in existential literature weakens the moral and spiritual imperatives of a loving God.

♦ Pragmatism fails to take into account the real implications of an afterlife and the prophetic messages dealt with by Biblical eschatology. John Dewey expressed a similar sense of material cause and effect with his instrumentalist philosophy. Like the Marxists, he also believed in a kind of Hegelian dialectic in the march of individual and collective existence. Yet, he did not believe in the dialectic necessity of history like Marx, nor did he believe in economic determinism. Although a materialist like Marx Dewey would be seen by Marxists as a 'bourgeois materialist', one who would see a world without the supernatural as the only real [sic] world, yet welcoming of middle class, bourgeois virtues.

♦ The "eat, drink, and be merry" mentality, or, in its updated form, "sun and surf" is cool, tries to bypass the rational and cognitive faculties and thereby pulls down education. In the high schools, we see the student emphasis on "hanging out," which really is reflective of the USA's undo emphasis on having a good time, and working throughout the week to get to T.G.I.F. functions at the end of the week. It is reflective of our sports manias, orgies of entertainment via live concerts, TV (hundreds of channels), and abandoned search for sexual satisfaction, getting high, or getting wasted in the bars. It's a pretty grim picture which all thinking people are, by now, aware of. Thus, hedonism fails.

♦ Materialism reduces man to his "thing-ness" or to biology, and thus denies the truth of humanity as also constituting soul and spirit. In the high schools, we need to resurrect teaching of the medieval philosophers like Augustine, Bonaventure, Boethius, Aquinas, Duns Scotus, and Abelard to begin to once again see humankind in its wholeness. The philosophies of Bergson, Dewey, Peirce, James, Santayana, Spencer, Hegel, Marx, Freud, Mill, and Bentham are doing irreparable harm and must be exorcised from the minds of the people.

♦ Atheism leads the curious and seeking mind into darkness and irreparable harm. In short, we are walking in doom insofar as our schools are houses of godlessness.

ONE REFORMER WE DO NOT WANT TO LISTEN TO: A COMMENT ON HOWARD GARDNER'S BOOK *THE DISCIPLINED MIND: WHAT ALL STUDENTS SHOULD UNDERSTAND*

Prof. Gardner's book is disappointing. He tries to be all things to all people saying both that he believes in basic competencies, but wants to put inquiry first. Also, his language is inflated, and lacking in philosophical specificity. For example, he believes in building up the inner world of "mental representations" [unexplained term] yet insists on "performances of understanding" [another unexplained term].

Also, he has respect for the individual learner and individual differences, yet he is concerned about the "position" or "situation" or social class dynamics in which the learning takes place. Thus, he fails to do justice either to the individual or to class, race, or gender. The role of leadership in learning is wholly ignored; and responsibility is not explored. In short, it is extremely difficult to pin down Prof. Gardner. It would be kind to say he is eclectic. One hopes it's just not fuzzy thinking.

However, we can discern that he has a romantic obsession with beauty, truth, and goodness. Imagine -- the Holocaust is reduced to being an illustration of what goodness is or is not! His treatment of these ideas is superficial and banal. One does not like to be so judgmental, but his writing about them does not deserve a detailed analysis.

When attacking E.D. Hirsch whom he calls the main speaker for "cultural literacy," he sets up a straw man. He says that Hirsch's school of thought has an underlying belief in the Lockeian "tabula rasa." Yet, there is nothing explicitly stated or implied in Hirsch's writings to indicate that he believes in a *tabula rasa.* Hirsch's main premise that there is a body of knowledge to be acquired in order to attain cultural literacy has nothing to do with whether or not there are innate ideas.

Further, is Prof. Gardner really less elitist than Hirsch as some have claimed? I have found that the Harvard elite spend their entire lives trying to achieve and learn everything, and be on top. Their lives are marked by ambition to the Nth degree; yet, he debunks time-honored and experience-honored content areas that traditionally have defined literacy at its best. Thus, there is a certain inherent dishonesty in Gardner's presentation.

Prof. Gardner has a romantic obsession with beauty, truth, and goodness. He is overly fixated upon John Keats' "Ode To A Grecian Urn" which undoubtedly he read in grade school. The key line which all educated students must explicate is "Beauty is truth and truth is beauty. That is all ye know and all ye need to know." While these words by Keats are exceedingly precious, it would be somewhat less than wise to elevate his thoughts to a philosophy of eduction suitable for the complex life of 21st Century humanity in the USA. Gardner continuously tells the reader that he is almost transported into ecstasy by creativity and moral engagement. Yet despite his almost hypnotic writing style, when one enters the actual substance of the book, one finds banality and uninspired thought patterns.

There is a tendency on Prof. Gardner's part to oversimplify certain issues like the Holocaust, and to overcomplicate certain others like the nature of intelligence. As the reader may be aware, he is the leading promoter of the idea of 'multiple intelligences'(not discussed in this book) that has attracted various reformers as a viable alternative to the traditional I.Q. concept. Suffice it to say here, there is almost no data to support his views on the nature of intelligence despite the widespread buy-in.

The world is not waiting for the concept of intelligence to be re-written. Is this writer oversimplifying when stating that there is something very awkward about saying that there is no fundamental difference in intelligence between Einstein and the custodian of my school? Is this awkwardness because I am an elitist putting down the custodian? Is it because of lack of intelligence that I am still in the grip of a univocal definition of intelligence? I don't think so. Rather, we all know we are dependent on each other, and that everybody has some unique aptitudes or gifts they can express and be respected for. However, trying to elevate this understanding to a higher level of truth or intellectual significance is illegitimate.

Lastly, his writing style is a bit too fond of adjectives, and the book reads as a whole like *It Takes A Village* by Mrs. Clinton. *The Disciplined Mind* has a mellifluous style that presents itself as being highly sophisticated and, at the same time, as down-to-earth, with balanced common sense. Yet, ultimately, the book is boring. As one Amazon reviewer states, Prof. Gardner is full of himself.

In this book, there is no straightforward discussion or emphasis placed on knowledge, critical, logical thinking, justice, Judeo-Christian values, persistence, responsibility, or character development...words which are essential for a true philosophy of education.

LETTERS TO A FRIEND
These letters were written to a young teacher who daily bemoaned the humiliations of teaching in the New York public high schools. He and I shared many deep conversations about teaching and the conditions of education as they now obtain. These are some thoughts that were shared with my colleague.

Dear Friend,

I think you and I agree on democratizing the public schools, and in many cases privatizing them in order to bring about greater democracy. Schools will have to be more effective and responsive to students and society if they want to continue earning money. It seems like a crude measure of reality; yet true.

What is reform? Unfortunately, some of the developments make me shudder. In one elementary school I read about in the *NY Times,* the teachers have a script from which they are to teach. Every day's lesson is programmed for the teacher, and even what they say to the students is written into a script. Every once in awhile, some nasty lady comes in and tells the new teachers they are deviating from the script. Gradually, if they do not quit, they are trained into submission to the script. When they conform to the script, they are praised for their "teaching potential" [sic].

Does the script produce better results? If it does, then parents might choose such a school methodology. Yet, the loss of freedom would be enormous.

School success might then mean an unbelievable micro-management of the classroom, and a rigid, almost totalitarian, approach to teaching. Failure will not be allowed. Is this loss of freedom really justifiable in terms of "success?"

Privatizing and charter schools may lead to more success in reading and math scores, especially for the early ages, but since we cannot see into the future, we must look at reform with a certain caution knowing that there may be dangerous, unforeseen consequences. And we have to remember that the system which now seems to be producing so much failure, especially in the big cites, and especially among certain minorities, is the same system in which tens of millions are still succeeding, and which has worked very well for a very long time. Further, privatized schools are more immune to public influence, and thus their mistakes might over time be more difficult to correct than the mistakes of public institutions.

So, I'm for privatizing, with qualifications.
Regards,
JL

Dear Friend,

I'm for merit pay in some settings, but not in New York, or most big city systems. Why? I am convinced that most (say 90-95%) of those receiving that bonus would receive it on the basis of politics. In my last school, a teacher was nominated for New York State Teacher of the Year (she won!), and she did not teach one course or class! She ran several programs and the resource room. My God! Friends and relatives of educational administrators would be first in line to receive bonuses.

It hurts not to receive some tangible reward when one knows one is working hard and succeeding in some ways that others are not; yet even more hurtful is seeing undeserving ones, or those with false beliefs receiving those rewards on a regular basis. I look at the s*takhanovites* of the Russian revolution under Stalin. They were his darlings. They had the energy to work seventy-two and eighty hours a week on big construction sites, with enthusiasm for the revolution even when sometimes for long periods of time they didn't get paid. They made everybody else look bad and feel bad. "Don't worry about fair treatment," they affirmed, "but think only of the Revolution." (Maybe you have already seen examples of this even though we are not under Stalin?...) These *stakhanovites* were killing themselves for a philosophy and a man that weren't worth a damn. The masses of people with possibly less energy and possibly more integrity than the *stakhanovite* workers died under the shadow of their "success." The *stakhanovites* were living a lie and enjoying it. The lie was, so to speak, "made for them," and their ability to function well under Stalin became a problem for everyone else, not only in Russia, but worldwide. The Soviet economy was built up, but humanity took a seventy-five year leap backwards because that sycophantic crew "succeeded."

Regards,

JL

Dear Friend,

Many special education students often tell their teachers, "This is special education, so I'm expected to act crazy." That's why there have been attempts to mainstream these youth. Only my experience has been that when they get mainstreamed they continue to "act crazy." They think the label is the source of their problem, but ultimately it is not. The whole tendency in schools has been away from tracking because they say studies have shown that when students who are low performers are exclusively tracked with others like themselves, they are more apt to become discouraged, to have a low self-esteem, and to accept failure. On the other hand, when they are put in classes with brighter or more cooperative students, they hold back the progress of the better ones. This is a leveling tendency in the schools, especially in the big cities. With this tendency, the brighter students become discouraged and cynical.

The new emphasis on cooperative learning is to allow the brighter students to help the lower per-forming students, and to allow the lower performing students to rise to a higher level of recognition because of the "success" of the group (reflective of the success of the brighter members of the group).

The only problem with this is that it does not work. There have always been group activities in classrooms, but to emphasize group work on a regular basis tends to destroy individual initiative; and my experience is that the more motivated and brighter students do better whether cooperative learning is the main methodology or whether a more traditional classroom methodology is used. The downside however is that there is a loss of higher levels of achievement by those individuals who could develop more under the traditional methodology. Despite the cooperative learning "cure all," in 20+ years of high school teaching, only one student told me that she believed she learned better in groups rather than individually. But I had numerous students bemoan groups because so many members of the group were not holding up their share of the work.

Regards,

JL

Dear Friend,

Continue to serve humanity. There are things business executives don't understand, even the President of the U.S.A. doesn't understand. The Bible says, "If you exalt yourself, you will be humbled, but if you humble yourself you will be exalted." Teaching can be such a self-humbling. The Bible says, "The Lord loves a humble and contrite heart." Also, "come to Me all you who are overburdened in your souls, for My yoke is easy and My burden light." Also, "I am meek and lowly of heart." What did you read from Thoreau today? -- I believe it said to "follow your genius." Well, someone better have his "genius" in order to follow it. Not everybody has that quality. Frank Sinatra said, "I did it my way...." That is good enough for the common man. But for the one who has the quality of "genius" it is necessary to follow a higher path of creativity, duty, responsibility, hope, and SERVICE.

A higher path is humbling. It breaks us. We can be low man or low woman on the totem pole. We can march to a different drum beat. It hurts to be a revolutionary without a constituency. It hurts to be an actor or actress always auditioning, yet never getting the role. It hurts to be the salesman who's always on the road, always reaching out; yet never doing better than just getting by. But the hurt can be borne...and it can especially be borne if we understand that God has called us to serve. And He has called you to serve. All this pain is leading you to Him! Yes. Seek and you shall find. Knock and it shall be opened unto you. Ask and you shall receive. Don't judge a job by status, but by the merits of the job as you see them. Yes, will you be able to meet your expenses? Will you be able to have health coverage? Is there any tuition package (do you really want to take more courses?)? But these practical questions, in my opinion, should come second. Forget about being an American materialist. Live to serve. Though it might sometimes seem otherwise, you are not alone.

By your actions, your intentions have been revealed to God, and more and more He will reveal His intentions to you. The psalmist says, "Tears come in the night, but joy comes in the morning." Read these priceless words dear colleague. Whatever I am telling you here comes from an informed and eternal relationship with Almighty God or, in Hebrew, *melech hagadol* [the Great King].

Regards,

JL

Dear Friend,

Some solutions for the educational problems of our society:

➢ More teacher caring and sensitivity to the needs of the **individual**.
➢ Expansion of privatization and charter schools.
➢ More orderly and disciplined schools.
➢ Greater variety of books in humanities courses. Less emphasis on textbooks. Textbooks with fewer graphics. Textbooks written by one or two individuals rather than by committees.
➢ Emphasis on morals and character building. Judeo-Christian values promoted.
➢ Full-scale war on corruption in management.
➢ The right people for the right jobs. (Typically, the Assistant Principals of Administration, in charge of school expenses and budgetary matters, never had one accounting course.)
➢ Teachers and administrators who are not obsessed with nor promoting new left ideology.
➢ Cleanliness and safety in buildings.
➢ Happiness, joy, generosity, mercy, strictness, integrity.
➢ Return of regular prayer in some form to all schools.

Regards,

JL

Dear Friend,

Once one is a caring person, then one sees how the attitudes, values, and institutional structures are all scrambled up and messed up. So, opportunities then arise for unscrambling and de-messing the situation, and we take them as they come. Some reforms we can initiate with the pen or with politics. Most reforms arise from tremendous personal sacrifice. The greatest reform is to remain a caring person in the midst of a tough and messy situation. Patience and endurance are two important qualities humanitarians need to cultivate. Look at Albert Schweitzer: he didn't put the voodoo witch doctors out of business, but he sure did a lot for the Africans by just hanging in there decade after decade. He was a light in the darkness. That's what we are when we are at our best. If we can remain in a created space of light, then we shall have done a great deal even if every blankety-blank educator and politician refuses to consider, discuss, and debate the new ideas we may have to offer. Amen.

Regards,

JL

THE IDEAS ARE REALLY FLOWING

1. Increase amenities for teachers – e.g. teachers' centers, lounges, vending machines, air conditioning, lockers, clean, well-maintained classrooms.

2. Provide a 20% across the board, one-time, no strings attached salary increase, nationwide, for all teachers. This will be society's way of saying WE LOVE AND APPRECIATE YOU.

3. Legislate a new national holiday: Teacher Appreciation Day.

4. Give bonuses for teachers based on consistent enthusiasm in the classroom and the ability to explain complex ideas.

5. Teach a greater variety of languages, including Asian languages for non-Asians.

6. Eliminate all bilingual programs. One language for one people irrespective of race or national origin!

7. Conduct anti-bullying programs, including assemblies, lessons, and school decorations.

8. Launch school-wide attempts to help adolescents in a wide variety of problem areas (see EVEN OSTRICHES KNOW WHEN TO RUN).

9. Eliminate whole language approaches to reading. Phonics is the only way to go.
10. Eliminate the "new math" and the "new new math."
11. Require business courses for all tracks, including the academic.
12. Return resources to true, hands-on vocational education.
13. Family values promoted – virtues, morality.
14. Expand privatization. We must do whatever we can to break the educational MONOPOLY we presently have which is socialism at its worst.
15. Expand charter schools but within a context of strict financial and educational accountability.
16. Go back to basics in all subjects and in all grades. See the writings of E.D, Hirsch on how to do this.
17. Establish acceptable reading standards for first grade, not for fourth grade.
18. Use textbooks with fewer graphics and more facts. The New New Left will tell you that there are no "facts" – only an amalgamation or consolidation of information within the context of an ideological bias. Remember, they believe in

radical relativism. It is radical in the sense that almost no objectivity exists, nothing can be known, and…therefore…anything can be taught! Forget about truth. Forget about balanced scholarship. Forget about intellectual honesty and integrity! Why? Because those concepts are themselves part of an institutional bias in favor of conservative, capitalistic values. The statists hate this bias!

19. Emphasize sexual abstinence outside of marriage and traditional heterosexual marriage as the precious ideal for intimate human relationships.
20. Stop distribution of condoms.
21. Stop abortion counseling in schools, and forbid abortion referrals.
22. Abolish abortion in society. No one is free to take a life. Abortion is sending a deadly message to all.
One cannot send the message that the schools care about kids when 50+ million babies have been killed in the greatest holocaust since the beginning of history. Those words of "concern" and "caring" must ring hollow.

23. Order and discipline must be restored where it is absent (almost everywhere).

24. Restore patriotism, especially in high schools and junior highs. This means love of country must be openly expressed by teachers and administrators at frequent gatherings of students, and there must be regular singing of the national anthem, recitation of the Pledge of Allegiance to the Flag, and singing of patriotic songs. Why would we wish to serve others and contribute to the lives of others if we do not see them as fellow citizens who are part of the same wider community as others.

25. Restore Bible reading to the public schools including and especially the Ten Commandments, the Sermon on the Mount, and the Lord's Prayer. There was a controversy in New York because a candidate for mayor, who is Jewish, said that he recited the Lord's Prayer when he was in school and thought that reciting that prayer would set a good tone in the schools. When criticized by Jewish groups who said that that prayer was a "Christian prayer" [sic], he quickly, and rightly

replied, "Nobody owns the prayer. It belongs to everybody and anybody who wants to say it."

26. Place more emphasis upon facts. The pendulum should swing back to rote work and what used to be called disparagingly "regurgitation." In today's schools, students resist using the terminology used by the teachers, and that is because they have been told for so long to "be creative," i.e., put everything in your own words and do not memorize. Yes, many teachers who are averse to teaching facts – they want to see students conceptualize. Yet, there is a certain dissociation in the thinking of teachers because, at the high school level, many are aware that the students lack the information they really need. Many teachers feel they are forced to choose between expecting facts (rote work) and, on the other side, getting the generalizations but not having facts. A lot of teachers today are choosing the latter even though they realize the inadequacy of that position. We teachers must switch gears and demand more facts even if, in the short run, some creative thinking is short-circuited (is it really creative or is it just

vacuous, "full of sound and fury, signifying nothing

27. Eliminate alternative assessments. Everybody has to secure his or her grade by the same measures as everyone else. Portfolios of student work conceived of on an individual basis are too subjective, and need to be abandoned. These portfolios are subject to excessive manipulation based on pre-set quotas for passing and for attaining higher grade levels in order to churn out impressive statistics. A more honest mindset in the authorities would of course have to accompany any change. *There has to be a change in the minds/hearts/souls of people, not merely policy changes in order for a restoration of educational quality to take place.*

28. Emphasize history and geography at all levels. Six credits of geography should be required for all teachers. All teachers should have at least twelve college credits of history.

29. Require study of European and American History, including laws, comparative governments, and intellectual history as well as political

and social history. Economics should be required
for every high school student in the United States.
30. Return schools to their original role as
educational institutions, and not as one-stop social
service centers.

THE COLUMBINE HIGH SCHOOL SHOOTING: AN HISTORICAL WATERSHED

Despite the chaos reigning in the urban high
schools, the most violent action and massacre of our
times in American high schools took place at
Columbine High School in the relatively upscale,
middle-class town of Littleton, Colorado. There is a
darkness in the land that cannot be contained or
attributed to urban life or the poor or to any ethnicity
or religion. The glow of narcissism can be found in
Columbine just as it is found in the high schools
where this writer taught in NYC. Permissiveness,
self-satisfaction, and self-righteousness can be seen
in the Columbine story. Narcissism is, of course, an
extreme of self-centeredness, and self-centeredness
as opposed to God-centeredness is sin.

Without having our lives lived before a holy
God – whereby we shall still be sinning but

acknowledge our responsibility for those sins – we can expect even more horrors and more terrors.

At Columbine, a courageous teacher gave his life for his students. We need more teachers willing to take a bullet for their students. But when this writer mentioned this thought to his students, I also added that that was not an invitation for you to come to school and shoot me.

The family of an African-American boy who was shot at Columbine eventually had to leave town because they dared suggest that there was a problem with the racial attitudes of the town and the school officials. We need to humbly pray to God to remove these dark attitudes of prejudice from our hearts.

A follow-up anniversary of the event was more of a celebration than a solemn memorial. The town leaders were rightly criticized for setting the wrong tone.

The killers had sometimes been bullied and ridiculed. Could issues of bullying and ridicule not be addressed? The boys themselves were members of the "black trench coat mafia." They gave the Nazi salute to each other in the school. Does this have to be tolerated? Too much is tolerated in Columbine and in schools throughout the nation, while at the same time we see paranoid overreactions where children are suspended for pointing their thumb and forefinger as pretend guns in the early grades.

Yet, clearly, true kindness, understanding, mercy, and compassion (which all require discipline as well as expressions of warm feelings) are in short supply. At the same time, students who have identifiable health problems are failed because "the performance is the only thing that counts." Harris and Klebold, the Columbine shooters, were clearly maniacs and responsible for the evil deeds of that horrible day. Yet, we know that high school and college shootings have increased in number dramatically since the 1970's. Sensitive, informed observers cannot help but observe that these decades followed the cultural and moral upheavals of the sixties and early seventies, the elimination of prayer in schools, the upsurge in civil disobedience, the exponential increase in drug use, the death of millions upon millions of babies through abortion. Combine this with our national failure in Vietnam, corruption in government, and the growing

ascendance of the Left domestically, we can see why
we are in such a dark and chaotic place today.

WHAT ARE THE ANSWERS TO THE
PROBLEMS FACING OUR SCHOOLS?

Violence in the schools. What's the answer?
The answer is peace, hope, and love. The answer is
a stronger family life for the students. The answer is
a strong Judeo-Christian morality inculcated into the
students. There cannot be true peace without love
(including discipline as well as tenderness). Peace
can only come through a moral code, a belief in
God, and prayer. Judeo-Christian morality must be
restored in the schools and in our culture. Prayer
must be restored to the public schools. If we are
"one nation under God" we can have a prayer
amendment without infringing on federalism. It
might even be a negative amendment to the effect
that states cannot be disallowed from having daily
silent prayers in their schools if they so choose. If
the idea of a God of the universe cannot be officially
acknowledged in the schools, then, for sure, whether
schools are privatized or remain public, education
and following that, society itself, is doomed!

Lack of student motivation to learn: The answer again is prayer, morality, and a return to classical educational values – great books should again be central to the curriculum as well as classical languages (Greek and Latin) and Hebrew. History books should suggest righteousness and patriotic values. Heroes should be identified. Achievements of our culture should be emphasized as well as shortcomings or failures. If Europe and the USA are as bad as the politically correct crowd proclaim, then is that not, at a deeper level, a reason not to be bothered learning what is taught? If Western Civilization and its values are taught as merely a gas station stop on the way to get a better job, then we are teaching based on extrinsic values, whereas there should be an emphasis on the intrinsic values of Western Civilization. In other words, learning for learning's sake is good insofar as we are becoming identified with the best that Western Civilization (not global civilization) has to offer.

Then we should consider the matter of published school statistics. Mayor Bloomberg, for twelve years mayor of New York City, with his brilliant financial services background, was a master manipulator in this area, aided and abetted by his long-time Chancellor Joel Klein. I taught in a high school where the entire cohort of schools being evaluated along with my school were set a goal that 85% of the students should receive 85 or higher on the NY State Regents. Over time, that shifted to 85% receiving an average score of 85 on the Regents. The better students found it easy to get 85 or higher, so the courses, which put a greater emphasis on the Regents, actually became too easy for the better students (which were a substantial proportion of the student body of this specialized high school). Meanwhile, the Regents became easier, so that many of the bright, but less than exceptional, students could also pass or get in the 70's, so this again -- with the emphasis on the Regents -- meant less concern among teachers and students about the courses themselves.

Further, Regents grades were pegged by the principal to count as 20% of a student's final grades. When I began teaching it was not allowed for the Regents to be part of a course grade, but the NY State Board of Regents during the Bloomberg years issued a waiver which allowed this practice. The net result is that statistics became an end in themselves, and learning went down especially among the more able students. I would encourage an end to this practice.

Previous to the present Regents requirements there were RCT exams for the less able students, and I taught in one high school with a high "at risk" student population. In social studies, in that school the Regents passing rate (with the easier RCT exams) was only 20-30%!!! Therefore, what kinds of deceptions are involved with all kids now taking the Regents exams (with Regents being written as more difficult than previous RCTs yet easier than Regents of an earlier era, say, ten years ago)?

The emphasis should be put upon getting more highly educated teachers in the classrooms -- graduates of more academically challenging colleges and universities. Further, the schools have to rethink the treatment of behavior infractions. The level of disobedience in the public schools is horrible!!! The arrogance of the youth is beyond almost anyone's conception.

Further, I would earnestly ask you to research why the Danielson method of teacher evaluation has been selected, and if it really provides the best parameters for evaluating teachers. Also, I hope you, dear reader, will re-evaluate the norming of statistics for determining which teachers are making the best progress in improving student test scores. First, the tests used to compare teachers will have to be properly normed, i.e., test questions will have to be used that have been properly normed and standardized in pilot testing situations, not based on any old test the principal or assistant principal happens to have in his/her drawer or computer. Second, variables in student backgrounds (socio-economic, race) should also include student lateness, truancy, cutting, and incidents of misbehavior, so that teachers who teach misbehaving, poor, minority kids are not given impossible hurdles of performance results to overcome. Students need to take some responsibility for their test scores EVEN FACTORING THAT RESPONSIBILITY INTO THE STATISTICS. If you put too much pressure on new teachers, that will be another reason for them to quit education and contribute to institutional instability.

Also, there needs to be more patriotism in our public schools. The schools are part of our cohesion as a constitutional republic. During my 20+ years in the high schools of NYC, not one patriotic song was ever sung in the schools! Only at graduation ceremonies was the "Star Spangled Banner" sung. Because of security issues in the high schools, there are few assemblies, but I suggest that there be more assemblies. I would have four assemblies instead of two, in order to accommodate the entire student body. In the smaller academy schools, assemblies are more feasible than they would be in comprehensive high schools. The students need to feel a greater sense of purpose that a sincere patriotism and appreciation of America will bring into their lives.

A sense of purpose in life can drive out all kinds of emotional negatives in the lives of people. Meriwether Lewis of the Lewis & Clark expedition was often afflicted by serious depressions, but his sense of purpose enabled him to successfully complete that amazing trek in the wilderness and write copious notes about the flora and fauna as well as the tribes he encountered.[22] Abraham Lincoln's melancholy and deep depressions have been admirably depicted by Joshua Shenk, and it is clear that his sense of purpose and love of country enabled him to function and go far beyond mere functioning despite his mental health issues.[23] Look at the inspiration of Joni Eareckson Tada who, though paralyzed from the neck down, was able to have a successful career, and even married.[24] Her sense of purpose and godliness carried her forward despite her seemingly impossible disabilities. These are reasons why patriotism and school spirit are so important.

The writings of E.D. Hirsch should be the basis for a Back-To-Basics reform of education.[25] Under his philosophy, there is a body of knowledge to be learned at every level. Education to fit a particular model of what is or is not a "healthy psychology" should be de-emphasized in favor of more legitimate academic goals (yet not out of reach

---

[22] Thomas Danisi, Uncovering the Truth About Meriwether Lewis, Prometheus Books, 2012.

[23] Joshua Wolf Shenk Lincoln's Melancholy: How Depression Challenged a President and Fueled His Greatness, Mariner Books, 2006.

[24] Joni Eraeckson Tada, Joni: an Unforgettable Story, Zondervan 2001.

[25] E.D. Hirsch, Cultural Literacy: What Every American Needs to Know, Vintage Books, 1988, as well as other writings by Prof. Hirsch.

of the abilities of the masses). Right now, the thinking of Abraham Maslow is in the ascendancy. To me, it is of dubious validity although it contains nuggets of insight and wisdom. However, using his writings as a sacred cow, I think that modern educators have overplayed the values of his "self fulfillment" system of values (he calls it a "values hierarchy" with self-fulfillment at the apex of the hierarchy).

Giving every student an iPad or mini-iPad may be good PR, but think of the costs of replacement and maintenance. This writer has seen students smashing keyboards of computers, putting crazy glue in mice or in the keys of keyboards, or throwing monitors on the floor. Having students do more work on their own with computers is a dream. If they won't work in a class where there is some pressure on them, they will work even less if they need to do more at home and less in school (as with iZone). Personnel who are implementing these innovations have a built-in incentive to say they are working great in order to keep their jobs and gratify the ego needs of their managers. What teacher is going to be working with a program for a year and say it sucks? Please have people in charge who understand some of these issues.

The curriculum for every subject must be reviewed by the best minds in conjunction with educators who are experienced working within specific communities, and with specific grades and levels of students. Why has this not happened? I taught in one school for six years – a so-called low performing school in New York City. The passing rate for NY State Regents exams – exams required statewide for students hoping to obtain a high school diploma – in these schools ran between 20%-30%. Scores as low as 50 were regularly "scrubbed" or even simply erased in order to raise the passing percentages, so that another 5%-10% could pass. Incredibly, in six years at that school, NY State which is responsible for reviewing the exam results never once cited the school for cheating in the grading of these exams. Even with such a low number passing, the results still represented, in my opinion, giving away the store. Yet, there was not ONE investigation!

Patriotic songs should be regularly sung through all years in high school. None are sung at any time in the high schools in New York unless you count the National Anthem sung at, and only at, graduation ceremonies. Family values should be promoted: sex without marriage should be portrayed as less dignified, less moral, less stable, and less satisfying than sex within marriage. Sex within marriage promises maximum satisfaction in intimacy. Further, marriage and procreation must be portrayed as the societal ideal, not only in "sex ed" classes, but whenever family is portrayed. Mothers' Day and Fathers' Day should be celebrated in the schools. Of course, foster mothers and fathers, adoptive mothers and fathers, and guardians who are acting as mothers and/or fathers should be honored as well on those days. Everyone should realize that they are surrogate moms and dads, and while their efforts may sometimes be heroic, the heroism is in part because they are not the 'real' mom or dad, but they care and strenuously support the young person as if they were. Do you dear reader know that there are millions of moms, aunts, and grandmas who are not preparing any breakfast for their children, nor are they packing even a sandwich or a piece of fruit for lunch? Did you know that there is a failure to give attention to and love many of the youth in our society? The school cafeteria providing breakfast or lunch cannot substitute for having a loving mom or mom surrogate make breakfast and lunch.

Drug taking should be portrayed as wrong. Excessive drinking should be portrayed as wrong. Pornography should be portrayed as wrong. Profanity should be portrayed as wrong. Crime is just that – crime -- and should be repudiated, hence the repudiation of any modern music that glorifies crime.

The family of man should be lifted up through cultural events, especially in our urban areas, where all cultures can share their pride in their food, dance, songs, architecture, poetry, drama, philosophy and religion, literature, paintings and sculpture. At one school where I taught there was a "culture day." But the "culture" was limited to clothing, carrying or wearing of that country's flag, and to dancing over-sexed dances from that country. At another school, there were also some samples of various national food dishes. All other manifestations of culture as listed above were ignored. Thus, we need cultural events that are not one or two dimensional. Two or more weeks can be set aside for a variety of exhibits and assembly programs depicting the entire range of contributions of various cultures to the USA and to the world.

Local control of the schools is necessary because of the unique environments in which schools exist. Some communities have more immigrants than others. Some communities have more persons of one ethnicity or another. Some communities are more agricultural; others are more involved with finance or manufacturing. Communities each have a different identity which, for the sake of national unity, must be accepted and respected by all. That's why the Tenth Amendment left education to the respective states.[26] Any attempt to do an end run around that Amendment undermines federalism, a key principal of the success of the U.S. as a country and as an example to others. The U.S. is the only country in the world where the central government was created by the local governments. In every other place, the central government established the

---

[26] The Tenth Amendment to the U.S. Constitution states, "The powers not delegated to the United States by the Constitution, nor prohibited by it to the states, are reserved to the states respectively, or to the people."

structure of the provincial or regional governments of those countries.

The schools in general and the high schools in particular, especially in New York City, reflecting the direction of American society as a whole, are anti-family (in 20 years of teaching, Mother's Day and Father's Day were not celebrated or even acknowledged in the high schools where I taught), anti-faith (New York City schools do not allow multiple religions represented by decorations in the schools at Christmas), anti-federalism (the new Common Core State Standards are a federal takeover of education), anti-privacy (Common Core will collect data on a massive scale about the students in our schools), anti-individualism (increasingly the "unwritten" Constitution is projecting a reality where 'collective rights' are replacing 'individual rights', i.e., rights as a member of a class of people – female/male, straight/gay, minority/majority), and, incredibly, anti-achievement (watered down content passes as knowledge).

Are we really committed to analytic and synthetic modes of thinking? [These were explained 2-1/2 centuries ago by Immanuel Kant.] Do we really care about teaching induction and deduction or the scientific method? Do more than a few understand the connection between art and science? Who is asking why students in a leading New York high school are assigned for summer reading *The Immortal Life of Henrietta Lacks* instead of a major novel in English or American Literature? Why are delightful or morbid popular books assigned instead of classics of modern literature by Aldous Huxley, Somerset Maugham, James Baldwin, Saul Bellow, Theodore Dreiser, Ernest Hemingway, or others? A colleague I know who is substituting regularly in the New York City high schools has told me that so many schools are teaching the so-called "literature of oppression," and great white authors are purposely excluded. This is not and never could be a path to reconciliation for society as a whole or for minority communities.

· Do students know about the growth of federal agencies throughout our history? Do they know that Americans did not pay any income tax until 1916 except for a couple of years during the Civil War? Do they know why freedom of speech, freedom of religion, and freedom of the press all appear in one amendment rather than several amendments to the Constitution?

The list of items that are not taught or are taught too superficially goes on and on and encompasses science, math, history, literature (including poetry), or language. Instead of studying "foreign language" – many of the school departments in New York City are now called LOTE (Languages Other Than English) in order not to hurt the feelings of students who might be put off by the thought that their home language is "foreign," or "less than American." Amiability once again substitutes for truth. No Gertrude, you are not a second-class citizen!

Made in the USA
Columbia, SC
02 May 2019